THE *SUCCESSFUL* LADY.

INSIDE OUT

TSL is all about interdependence:

to rely on one another.

That's our true vision and mission with this organization.

We found our interdependence in you, and so will you.

Together towards success.

Yours truly,

The founders of TSL.

Förlag: BoD – Books on Demand, Stockholm, Sverige.
Tryck: BoD – Books on Demand, Norderstedt, Tyskland.
ISBN: 9789176992685

During this time, while writing this book, I have looked into my mirror. My mirror reflected the answers I needed when I was lost; the answers were given from my reflection. And this is me speaking, talking to my mirror. Can you hear me? Can you hear me, my better half.

ABOUT THE TSL-ORGANIZATION:

The TSL-organization is built on the mission to significantly increase the awareness in every woman, to make her understand her capacity, capability and belief, even in a dynamic world where we tend to loose more and more of ourselves. It all lies within her. We just want to bring it up to the surface – together – so we end up loving and respecting the one in the mirror.

www.tslorganization.com

BEHIND THE SCENES:

People have closed ones. People tend to be around people who can relate to them – aspects that relate to one another. People with similar values and beliefs are highly preferable, this since they put significance in the same aspects. This is how cultures and cults were formed: beliefs in the same aspects. Human beings put faith in whatever they value, as well as belief in a better future. But that better future does not come without a cost, does it? To fulfill your values and beliefs, you need to work toward fulfilling that belief, which will increase your own value. Since I was a child, I was seldom amongst other children. I was shy, caused by different occasions that traumatized my well being. Having this in consideration, I only had value for one person in this world, and that person was unfortunately not me. It was better half. She was the one I valued, and the one that believed in me. Since I was little, I always admired her charisma. Usually twins can be jealous of one another, but in my case it was never jealousy: it was admiration. I learned from her. I observed and analyzed how everyone reacted in her presence, and took it all in consideration for developing a better *me*. That is why I valued her: she made every person feel like they were the most important person in her life. Including me. Even if I know that I am one of the ones she loves most in this world, I admired her character. She was so genuine, so real. This made me realize that I do not need to put on different facades or roles just to fulfill others needs. This made me realize that the one that needs to accept me was myself: the person in the mirror. See, one thing she taught me when I was twelve years old was one of the most important lessons: the reason people loved her was because she was empathic, yes, but what increased people's respect was her self-value, self-confidence and most importantly, her *self-respect.* Her confidence started with her inside, which is what she tried to teach me. But back then I was insecure. During my childhood I was narrow minded, thought everyone was against me. Even though I have many skeletons in my closet, what I did to myself was worse than what the environment did. Even if they pushed me down, I decided to stay down. So I chose to react rather than being proactive. Unfortunately, this happened more than once. But she was always there, picking up the pieces. Ready to help me regain belief in me. Ready to make me see my own value. Which I saw. Repeatedly. Build, and destroyed, and then built again. Everything to fulfill their needs. This was my childhood experience in short. But, her reflection never changed. And eventually, I learned to form my own reflection, with both self-belief and self-value. Even though my environment dragged me down, I taught myself to be proactive and work towards it – to overcome it all, to show what I am capable of. But here is the thing: I showed *myself*. She was my cause to start believing, which is why I needed to be around her always. She gave me strength, until I found my own strength. She was my cure, until I found it within. And she was my mirror, until I found my own reflection close to hers.

Here is the deal. I was insecure and my whole childhood went by looking for my true identity. With other words, I had identity crisis, constantly trying to fulfill the needs of others, where I always ended up sadder than the day before. Facades, roles, masks. I never knew what to do to be the one people admired – not knowing that being yourself is what will be admired by the right sort of people. This is what she taught me. I needed attention, not knowing that it was my attention to myself that I subconsciously searched for. I needed value, not knowing that I was looking for self-value. And I craved for love, not knowing that it was the love of myself that I was lacking. I wanted to fulfill everyone else's view of me, not knowing that I lost my self that way. But in the end, I got aware of it all. When I gained self-awareness, I also went thru hardships to deal with leaving the bad habits behind. It is always hard to move forward, make no mistake of it. It is hard, but it is not impossible and it will all be worth it in the end. I got to express myself this way, where I got to know my self. Within me, I have now a place where I go to whenever I need inspiration, peace or solutions. This place gives me answers to yet unknown questions. That is the power of what is within, and having a rock to lean against whenever I feel lost, that is another reflection of my favorite person. Happiness in whole is to have her close since she is my power, force and energy. Having her afar is, on the other hand, sadness on a complete different level, where it helps me regain my strength in my capabilities and myself. So having her afar helps me regain myself, and having her close helps me deal with the environment. But here is the thing, when she is close, I get inspired by the happiness, and when she is afar, I get inspired by my sadness. In whole, I always win. Since life is full of ups and downs, this is the way I deal with the cycle. Inspirations does not merely come form one emotion, it comes from all the emotions a person can feel. So this way I get inspired by different emotions and occasions, where they all strength me in one way or another. Hardships and benefits mold me to the one I today am, and I am continuously growing. Continuously fighting. So in the end, she is the place I call common ground, where she helped me set up my own values and beliefs. No matter if we are close or apart, her closeness or absence will always inspire me: the emotions she leaves behind do their part – and that is the reason why I keep fighting for my rights. Simply because I have found my peace in myself – merely because I had a rock to lean against whenever I felt lost. This made me fight for me. After all, what is worth the price is always worth the fight. Right?

MY BETTER HALF:

My heart goes out to you, my better half. This book and this organization are all thanks to your belief in me. Therefore, I want to begin this book by thanking you openly. Thank you for your belief in me, and thank you for your fighting spirit. That fighting spirit helped me see what you have been seeing all along. Thank you for believing in me, when I did not do it myself. Thank you lovie, from the bottom of my heart.

I used to think I was bad with words. How wrong could I have been? This last years showed me that I was everything but that. I was apparently good with words, I just did not know how to put them into disputes. I just did not know how to put them into sentences so you got the sense, feeling and emotion I wanted you to get. But I was mistaken. Apparently I could. Everyone can. I did not know it back then, but today I do. Better late than never I guess. I seldom expressed myself with the spoken words either, not until recently. I preferred expressing my feeling the non-verbal way. It was easier, simpler and less judgmental. However, the person that took me beyond these borders and made me feel in a complete different way was you. My love for you goes beyond the spoken words and beyond what the eyes can see. Like the painting "Mona Lisa" by Leonardo Da Vinci, is our love internal: you cannot put a prize on Mona Lisa and therefore, you cannot either put words or sight into my love for you. Those words would not make the love I have for you fair. The reason I think why my love for you is too big to either be seen or spoken of is because everything we get to feel is far bigger than anything else we can put our wisdoms on. So to love you, I needed to focus on my feelings and emotions, since I could neither taste, see, hear nor speak about it. Yes, our love goes beyond the human species too, it goes beyond space and even beyond the Universe. You are my special one, the one I have been blessed with.

Something bigger than us two, something bigger than anything else on planet Earth, decided to give me a gift, a gift I have been cherish every second of my life. You have been taking care of your sister during her hard times, where you made sure to let her know that she was not alone in this. I was not alone in this, I know it now. I was never alone. Since day one have I been blessed with you by my side. So I dedicate this book and my future to you. You helped me regain my belief in me multiply times, and now it is my turn to regain the belief in the future successful ladies to come. You became my power, my force, my inspiration and my shelter. Yes, you also became my reason to keep fighting and keep breathing. You became my life so I end this by saying: I love you beyond the spoken words, beyond what the eyes can see, and beyond infinity.

Thank you my better one, you have helped me. Now, together, we will help the next ones to come.

Take into consideration that this is from my experiences and my perspective. I write from personal experiences as well as personal learning's. What you read throughout this book is my personal and self development.

INSIDE EVERY DIVERGENT MIND

Identity is what defines "us"; how we as individuals see ourselves and how our environment sees and defines us. What would you do if you all along have been physically and mentally mistreated? What would you do if you in your entire childhood have been hearing from different sources that you were not enough? Well, when you come out from those occurrences, you are implemented by those thoughts and you seem to be wired in that way too, to always doubt yourself and your abilities. Believe me when I say, I have been there. People in my surroundings mistreated me so badly that I became so insecure that I did not even want to be seen. I usually had my hair down, protecting my body and face and used it as a shelter, to protect myself from harm, everything so people would not look at me (or I at least hoped nobody noticed me). I grew up this way, where I departed myself from the social interactions completely, creating a social phobia on my own. I grew up this way, where my sister became my shelter and I her shadow. That is how I saw myself – a shadow. Is that not absurd? Which person manipulates someone else into thinking less of herself? I kept on doing everything to impress these people, but they always saw my flaws instead. I kept building up facades to be the one they wanted me to be. I kept using roles that were acceptable by them, not realizing I was loosing my true self that way. They focused on my cons, while I wanted them to be proud of my pros. And of course, as a child, you think it is your fault and you go into a defence mood and since the surrounding highlighted the bad parts, you seem to do it too. You get influenced. You get prejudiced by their words and start to believe in them too. So I started to become the one their words made me, not realizing that I created a mask harder than stone. Underneath that stone face, I was drowning in emotions, but how many saw that?

This is the power of influence. Use it in negative matters, and you will change a person's life in negative ways. Use it wisely, and we will have a future worthy living in, with people that deal with their inside. Making sure to become one that stand for people's well being – focusing on their mental health is what the TSL-organization stands for: to increase people's awareness of their own mental health, as well as helping the one next to them. In order to help another human being, you need to help yourself first. In order to help yourself, you need to get to know yourself. And in order to getting to know yourself – to fully know yourself – and to break free from those doubting patterns, it requires effort, time and most importantly, *will*. That is how you will stand as a Victorian and your true identity will be found. But do not think for a second that it will be easy, and foremost: do not underestimate the power of influence – both from within and from without. So, my identity equals me. An identity I continuously work with every single day, because I know how hard it is to stay in focus: to not fall back into those doubting patterns. That is why I am here for you. I want to be able to help you, simply because I found comfort from my rock and shelter. She protected me when I needed her the most, and when I felt lost; she helped me re-gain my confidence. In the book, I might refer to her as "my better half" or "sister". Ladies, I want to be your rock, your mirror, and your Dr. Dre to your Eminem.

So, to end this section, I am asking you: *How come I was so insecure but nobody saw it while I was working in silence? How come I changed my view of myself? And how come I succeeded?* –There is actually one answer to all of these questions: Improvements and persistence. I built confidence and let it take time. But my better half was what made this possible. She helped me find that belief I had in me. She helped me regain trust and faith in me by being there for me – by showing support as well as showing me what I am truly capable of. This made me see myself from a complete different point of view and from a complete different perspective and angle. This made me fight for my rights simply because she lit up that fuel in me. That fuel that tackled all the demons my mental illness brought with. So yes, I want to help you with your confidence, belief and fuel. I had one. I was lucky. Now, while holding in this book, you are lucky as well. Someone believes in you, and I will, with all my power and force, help you realize how much you are worth.

So, take your time. Whenever you are ready.

We take it in your steps, together. You and me!

Welcome to TSL where family means comfort; comfort to take the next step together; together towards tomorrow's interdependence.

When you dream it, you become it; when you visualize it, you will live it. How?

By working hard towards fulfilling every goal of that vision.

19

Before diving into the Part 1, I want you to consider something. The first part is a bit long but if you want to have the fully understanding of my background, as well as the contextual as whole, these pages would be useful for you. However, if you choose to not read the introduction, you can turn to part 2, and dig into what the first chapter has to offer.

PART 1

WALKING DOWN THE MEMORY

LANE

START WITH YOUR MIRROR

The problem today is that, even though women, as much as men, have the rights to follow their dreams, there is many of us that actually do not follow thru with ours. How is it, that some women do not have the gut to follow their visions or what their hearts really wants and desire? And more importantly, are you one of those women? We believe that – even though these women have all the possibilities needed and required – what a woman first needs to deal with is her inner self. We strongly believe that we need to get to know the woman in the mirror and her *self*, before having the guts to push her towards achieving her dreams and visions for her future. With self-belief, you would not be destructed as easily to doubts in your surrounding. With belief, you would not get as influenced as you would have if you did not have belief. So, what the TSL-organization do believe is that a lady creates opportunity for herself firstly after she have been dealing with her inner self and getting to know *her*, where this knowledge will lead to her acknowledging her true calling in this world and therefore having the guts to face the world.

Since the environment, society, friends and family are all influences by former prejudices and stories, do we need to be in alliance with our inner self to be able to go after what we want. If we are not in alliance within, the outside forces will have their ways of wrapping their tentacles around our beliefs and kill them smoothly, creating their own beliefs in its place. As we will tell you throughout our existence, we might be the generation with the most possibilities, but with mental illnesses in this amount, it rather breaks us apart. Try to focus on what you have within, and you will find your true patterns outside those doubts. Try to focus on your dreams and wants, and you will find your own way out of those doubting patterns. In short, focus on eliminating the mental illness that you hold, and you will in turn see all the beauty that life has in store for you.

But, in order to do this, you need to be curious, you need to be willing to accept to yourself that there is something missing in your life and that you need to find out what it is, even if its going to put some true facts on the stand: you need to clean out *your* closet!

No barriers, no boundaries on what you can accomplish with the belief in yourself. Enlighten the fire in you!

TWO QUESTIONS TO ASK YOURSLEF BEFORE DIVING INTO THE BOOK:

Do me a favor and ask yourself two questions: *"How am I feeling today?"* and *"What is the meaning of my life?* After answering those questions truthfully, keep on reading to see my answers to the same questions.

In a world dominated by social media, it is easy to feel like everyone else is living a perfect and happy life just by looking at the posted pictures. Not taking the filters, shadowing or lighting into consideration. In fact, people nowadays are feeling lonelier than before, and therefore protect their misery behind a posted picture, which simply means that they solely are living for the posted pictures – to make them perfect for everyone else to see. We all want to be the one in our posted picture and therefore get lost in the illusion of a perfect world, everything so we loose track of the real world and our true beliefs, thoughts, emotions and feelings. How many of us – in the last month – have actually taken a pause in our daily routes and asked ourselves the question: *"How am I feeling today?"* Even if we did, would we dare to answer the question truthfully? Would anyone even care to listen to the answer?

26

Would we admit that our "real" self is not matching the one in the posted pictures? We all have a desire to be congruent with our selves – to feel that we made it to actualization. In order for us to reach there, our ideal self (how we want to be) must match the actual self-image (how we see our selves). But if you do not know yourself, then it is a mismatch (incongruence) between these two and when these mismatches happens, you most likely dislike the person in the mirror and you start live for having a perfect picture and life in general for everyone else to see, even though the mirror reflects the true story. And when you start living for the person on social media, you start feeling lost, where you always feel like you are putting on a mask – everything to achieve the society's expectations of you having it all. You simply intake a role. You feel untrue to your self, this because social media is putting pressure on you to become "perfect" – which causes stress and anxiety. But please, do not feel lost in the sea of social media. Life in general is not perfect and you have been given shoes that fit you. We all have felt lost, some more than others, where we felt like we are not fitting in in this world. Honestly speaking, in order for you to be true to your self – and be congruent with yourself – you need to stay honest with your self. Life is not perfect, and in order for you to face the obstacles on your path, you need to be fair to the one reflecting back. By the way, it is OK to cry. Cry a lot! Show emotions and show feelings! And I am here to tell you that I care about the answer. So let us try one more time: *"How are you feeling today?"*

To be able to answer the second question, you will need to elaborate the definition of the answer you have towards the question *"What is the meaning of life"*. The reason why is because the answer will be different coming from different people, which is the beauty of life. Different people will answer the question differently, dependent on their self, their surroundings, their vision and their view of the world. Being a successful lady increases the fulfillment of answering this question since you have taken one step toward being honest with yourself. What is the meaning of life? –Well, for me it was not to get into a relationship with an external part as soon as I got out of high school. I was too busy getting into a relationship with myself to have any time or effort for someone else. It was not going to University either, for I did that to make my parents proud. However, University taught me a lot about true knowledge in life, which is why I consider my University years my downfall as well as my rebirth. It was not getting any random job thrown at me either, since I wanted to find that environment where I could focus on increases in my character – rather than being neutralized. However, what I did for *me* was developing me toward a better version of my *self* – daily. I did this by constantly digging into my inner self and got to know the real me.

So if you ask me the question *"What do you think is the meaning of your life?"* I will simply answer: giving my future successful ladies and my self the treatment our bodies and minds deserves. I want to be someone people can relate themselves to, someone who makes them understand that they have all the tools indoors. I want them to understand that it all lies within, rather than being too busy with the outside facades. I want them to understand that happiness comes from the alliance with your self, rather than the alliance with the environment. I want them to understand that they do not need the environment to regulate their feelings and emotions. What they need is the love for themselves. I want to bring something to the world too, simply by helping women who are in a position where I have been. I simply want to be a role-model, for I have had one. I want to be a support to someone who has negativity surrounding them, for I have been there.

Knowing that this book can make them escape those daily routines and lives – and work towards fulfilling the meaning of their lives – is what this book and the TSL-organization is all about. Here is the thing: the meaning of *my* life is to give you the opportunity to change yours, the way my sister implemented on mine. She made me focus on my character: inside out. The meaning of my life is simply to give back. I want to give back by helping people who are in a position were they need help by an external part, or people who just lost their "true" identity or character in one way or another – which can happen easily when insecurity is lurking in the dark, especially in today's society. I had the privilege to be given a sister that helped me develop my self to the better version of me. Staying in this state of mind is something I fight against daily. Yes, it is a daily process since I need to push myself into continuous positive thinking because it is so easy to just fall back into those self-doubting and insecurity paths. I simply make sure to always increase my self in any way – by searching into my soul and always focusing on improving my self and my mind. So, my answer towards the question *"What's the meaning of my life"* in short will be: "The meaning of life is to help the person next to me with the knowledge I possess – not compete with one another, but help. And always do my best to be a great neighbor. Interdependence is the key to success. But first, help yourself. To be able to help others, you need to be in one piece yourself first. That is the meaning of *my* life!"

THE POWER OF SELF-RESPECT

How come, wherever I go, people look at me with respect without me even opening my mouth? How come I get this respect, even though they do not know a thing about either my background nor whom I am? – Well, the answer is simple; it is all *in your talk, your act, your behaviour and your thinking,* and if you stick with me throughout this book, I will show you my tricks that will indeed be useful to you, whether it is to get respect from yourself, your neighbour, or just show the world what you have to offer.

So, shall we begin?

Good, let's turn the page!

LOOK DEEPER WITHIN:

"Do not look in the rear-view mirror for too long – you might be stuck in that position. Change towards the road ahead. There is a reason why this window is bigger – make sure to put your whole focus there so you do not loose out on aspects coming your way. Therefore, be aware. Therefore, look deeper within. Therefore, find the one you were destined to be."

Everything starts with accepting yourself and your true destination, as well as realizing the fact that you do not have to be unhappy just because "certain aspects" did not go as you hoped. You can actually live the life that *you* want, no matter your background. Because you need to know one thing: it is never about what you just see, it is rather about what you think and believe regarding these matters. To be someone and to get somewhere in this world, you firstly need to change *your* view of yourself. Secondly, change the opponents' focus, which is primarily done by changing the focus on *what* you yourself focus on. What you put your focus on will be what everyone else does too, which is why you will need to switch your mindset first, before being able to change everyone else's view of you.

Why do we judge the book by its cover? This was a question I never knew the answer to when I was younger, yet I acted the same. I came to experience the answer to that question though. We do it all the time, judge the cover that is. How many people have been looking at books and chosen the book with a better cover, only to find the book really boring? Or how many have just taken a book, with a random cover or "no cover" at all, only to find the book amazingly good? Well, this is something we all teach our kids but do we believe in it ourselves, or more importantly, are we doing as we are teaching someone else? –The answer is no. If we would not judge a person by her cover, meaning the talk, you would not have the feeling of need to change. Instead of focusing on outside aspects, I want you to focus on what their inside is, namely their thinking, behaviour and action. And when it comes to the book, focus on what the story tells you, instead of how beautiful the cover is. By focusing on the inside aspects, you will see the outside as a reflection of their inside and therefore focus on the context instead. However, I want you to understand that I do not say that every good outside is empty or boring on the inside, make sure you hear me. I am simply saying that sometimes, the cover can be judged wrongly. Additionally is this book more than 'how to appeal to people' – it is more about how to find *you* and how to *appeal to yourself,* as well as how you break free from your doubts and your mental illness. It is about your birth and how to take advantage of the new you in the best possible way. For if you embrace the new you, the environment will do the same.

When you know why you are on planet Earth – when you know what your true calling is – it will be shown in the way you are acting, and your view of the world will be different. Take it from someone who has been where you are right now. By simply changing the view of yourself and the world, you will be acting differently and the people in your surrounding will be able to see the difference in you. Your children will be able to see it. They will be able to see that you act in line with your words and therefore mimic these actions, simply because actions speaks louder than words. However, it is safe to say that people do the opposite because that is how we got taught. We got taught from our parents, friends, neighbours and the environment we grew up in to judge the book by its cover, which they learned from their parents and their environment and so the story goes. This is all based on what they did to fit in. For example, why is it that the "outsiders" have a hard time during high school? – It is all affected by their cover. Meaning, how they looked. Just because they decided to not put a lot of time into thinking about what to wear or where the next party is, but put effort into their specialties and inside, did their time in high school get harder than it could have been. However, these people are usually the ones ending up with success and the reason is because, instead of putting effort into thinking how to be cool, what to wear and who to date and what to say to be "it", did they focus on giving fuel to what they believed in. No matter if the environment told them otherwise. These are the ones we all should cherish. These are the ones that dared to do what they loved, even though they did go through the hardest time: "judgy" high school. If we all would have followed and listen to our words instead of them being "empty words", we would have been as the "outsiders" in high school. But we do not and therefore do we become followers of "judge the book by its cover".

Children are good at observing and imitate their idols, which usually are their parents in their early years. Children notice more than you might think and they usually get the feeling fast on how *you* see yourself and the others in your surrounding, which are behaviours that they will in turn imprint and use themselves. So, if you judge the book by its cover, they will do the same thing. Remember that body language – non-verbal communication – speaks louder than words. But, *what is the correlation between the TSL-organization and this example?* – The correlation is that we *DO* judge the book by its cover simply because what we see is what we think they are. What people judge you for is your outside, meaning your communication. But we want to take this further. To be able to be someone that not only looks successful, but also feel successful, we need to dig deep within you and focus on your thinking, behaviour and your act. We want to give those "empty words" your definition of your cover. With other words, if you are confident, it will be shown in your posture, gestures, walk and behaviour. If you are insecure, this will be shown in the same way. So even if you have a great outfit but are feeling insecure with what you are doing with your life, this will be radiated and that aura will shadow the outfit you picked for the evening – and your book will be nothing but a cover. What I am applying is that we judge the book by the way they dress and walk, and therefore tend to lean against the people who are secure in their skin. By changing our inside toward the better, will we be able to radiate a better us, which will be judged correctly. That would make you a successful lady and that is what this book is all about.

WHAT DO I MEAN WITH THE TERMS "SUCCESSFUL" AND "LADY"?

Before being a successful lady, we need to know what the terms "success" and "lady" really means. So, what is the definition of a "lady", but also what does "success" really mean? Is success only about money I may ask you? Before diving into these definitions, I want you to ask yourself: is success only about money and if not, what more does it include? However, I also want you to ask yourself: what is a lady per definition? And please, do not look into the Internet; try to do this alone, just you and me.

Now, after writing it down or memorizing it, I will start by mentioning that success can be seen *not* only around money but everything else too; it is everything we accomplish. It is our own wealth. If you do not believe me then I will give you an example. You are a student that studies hard toward finishing your first year at the University. You study, study and study and finally do the test. If you pass the test, what do you call it? Do you not call it success? Exactly, that feeling after accomplishing a specific goal generates the feeling of success. Still not satisfied? I will give you another typical example. Whenever you want to loose weight, you start on a diet and do cardio regularly. Eventually you will loose weight and that is one type of success too. Success is the feeling we get after we gradually improve or accomplish something.

On the other hand, what is the definition of a lady? Are you right regarding that? First of all, what is a lady to you? You might associate ladies with snobby, unfriendly, unrespected and old-fashioned women that looks down on the people who have less money than they do. Maybe you associate a lady with the upper class in the movie *"Titanic"*, where they even look down on the people with "new money". However, this is not my definition of a lady. A lady is a woman who is respectful, kind and openhearted: someone who has sympathy and simply is down to earth. But a lady is more than that: she is a woman that maintains self-confidence. The duchess of Cambridge, Oprah, Michelle Obama and Anne Hathaway are four people that I associate with "a successful lady". These ladies are kind, helpful and confident. But are we forgetting something? Maybe the most important points: or actually *the* most important point. See, being a lady means that you have respect toward yourself first, so called self-respect, and that you have dignity toward yourself, but also a type of class, which you gain when you have respect toward both yourself and all other species. This will, in turn, lead to having etiquette in your actions because you know you and therefore act like you in your best manners.

The road from a woman to a lady is empowering, where personal development toward the best version of you is in focus. You need to learn to value aspects in life. You need to learn to know *you* to the fullest. Only then will self-awareness not be any problem since you know your boundaries and cells from head to toe. This shows that, to become a true lady according to our definition, you need to be dealing with your inside first, before you focus on your outside. Trying to feel like a lady without being through self-development is simply like having a birthday without a birthday-cake; you will know that there is something missing. Throughout this book I will give you advices to how to master yourself, with the mission towards becoming successful in your desiring area. If you follow these advices – both the aspects you shall highlight and those that you shall avoid – the result will be the same for all of you. But this only if you continuously work with your self by putting your heart, soul and emotions into it.

This book is divided into four chapters, excluded the introduction and conclusion parts. These chapters are: Think, Behave, Act, and Talk. There is a reason for this direction and you will find it throughout the book. The chapters will include what you already interpreted by reading each of the headings, which are written from my point of view. This book will additionally show you the importance of communication, where people judge by their first impression, which is usually made by the non-verbal communication. The non-verbal communication is one of the strongest communication skills people use since it gives a perception of the person without her even opening her mouth. But, the communication that is the most important one, and the one TSL-organization highlight, is mainly the communication between your mind and your body.

Before diving into the following chapters, I want you to read the sentences in the coming page and make sure to understand it fully. However, I also want you to take each chapter into consideration and see the value of each part, since these tricks can simply change your today by replacing some of your routines with the ones from this book. This is done by starting with looking into what I have to say; by getting an insight into what I have learned since I first started to truly know myself.

I will end the introduction-chapter by saying:

WELCOME TO MY REALITY AND YOUR FUTURE.

Become the master of your own destiny. You can make people see what you want them to see. The only thing you need to do is to change their perceptions, which can only be done if you change your own perceptions first. By changing your directions and your view of yourself, you will then be able to change your situation – it all starts with your view of yourself. By becoming the writer of the chapters in your own life, you can get the tomorrow you secretly or openly dreamt of. And remember, it is not just a thinking – it is access to a higher life – your perception and your future! Additionally: Always remember that these things take time. Getting to know you takes time, and getting to know your capabilities should be something you shall be persistent about: something you should be excited about. Remember that unlocking something within, that you have locked away, takes time, emotions and effort to change. And as I always say: "If someone gives me a specific hour for something like this to be done, I sincerely hope they go and to hide somewhere (metaphorically speaking). You cannot put time on perfection. Which means, you can not put your development towards becoming a lady on a hurry!"

PART 2

LOOK INDOORS. YOUR ACTOINS REFLECTS THE REAL YOU – YOUR THOUGHTS & BEHAVIOUR REFLECTS THE YOU WITHIN.

"Success is not a destination, but the road that you're on. Being successful means that you're working hard and walking your walk every day. You can only live your dream by working hard towards it. That's living your dream"

– Marlon Wayans.

THINK

"Mastering others is strength. Mastering yourself is true power" – Lao Tsu.

This chapter is the first one and will go through the environment, the mindset, the knowledge and other aspects you need to have in consideration to get the result you wish for. One thing to bear in mind is that this chapter goes hand in hand with the "behaviour" chapter, since the "think"-part is influenced by the behaviour and vice versa.

Notification: Something to have knowledge of before diving into the first section of this chapter – namely the environment – is that a lady commits herself into developing her mind to the better. She always develops to the best version of herself, and therefore always tries to develop the way she thinks. This makes her a person worthy success, simply because she fights for her independence, her rights, and her knowledge: humbly because a lady wants to make a mark.

"Progress is impossible without change, and those who cannot change their minds cannot change anything" – George Berard Shaw.

Now when we've enlightened the lust in you, let's turn the page and keep reading!

FIND THE RIGHT ENVIRONMENT FOR YOU AND YOUR TRUE CALLING.

To be able to succeed as a lady, you need to be in the right environment. Something to keep in mind is that, for a star to be born, it needs the right elements. So for a successful lady to be born, you need the right components as well, which includes being in the right environment. Therefore, my question for you is: *Are you happy in the society and in the environment you are living in today?* With other words, *do you think that that is the environment you belong in?*

"It takes time to find where you belong – but you need to give it just that: time".

By giving yourself time to find the right location for you, you will as a result also find your true calling in life, where greatness is accessible. The reason for this is because, as we mentioned above, you need the right components to bring out the special you, the *you* that focuses on what you are best at and enlighten that part in you. This goes hand in hand with both behaviour and actions, since you need to take action if you want to be someone and make it somewhere. *You need to think, then behave and act.* Unfortunately, many people do not have the guts to go after what they desire. These people do not dare to act, which will result in them being neutralized. Me, for example, have learned from this mistake. Today, I am trying to do the things that I love; I am putting myself first. I do not want to do things I am not comfortable with, which

48

you should not either. I am aware that some of you ladies out there has parents that decides your careers, which you feel obligated to follow since they are your parents and have been taking care of you since your birth. But, here is a thought: it is a parents' job to take care of his or her child. Your job, on the other hand, is to raise your children, and do you want to be the one deciding their lives? Making them live a life that you have in store for them? No, you probably do not because that is their life and they are in charge for their own lives, as you are of yours. Never think that you are forced just because you feel obligated. And I know that this is easier said than done, I am aware but I changed mine. Even though my parents wanted me to choose another direction in my academic career, they could not be prouder of my decision. And I just want you to know that yours will too, sooner or later, since they want you to be happy. True fact: most parents' want what is best for their children and if you make a solution based on your happiness, they will be happy for you as well.

To take this further, there is a lot of things you can realize if you only try to put yourself in the opponents shoes and try to understand why they acted the way they did in certain occasions. My closed ones' reason for acting the way they did was because in their mind, those actions were the right ones simply because that was the way they got treated. They were shifting their anger towards me, where they needed to release their tension somewhere. And since I had a habit that they disliked, they used that as an excuse. One explanation towards their actions could be that they thought in those terms because they saw these actions in their surroundings while growing up, and we tend to both imply and mirror the actions we see. So the environment treated them ill, which in turn led to them acting the same way in other occasions – and that, ladies and gentlemen, is how powerful a person's environment is. So technically, this could have been an act from the environment they grew up in – I just happened to revolt when I got older. Just remember, never become something else for someone else, no one will regret it more than you in the end. It is your life, make sure that you are the one holding the pencil and write your own chapters.

Where do you belong? Do you know it yet? This is a question that is hard to answer. Me for example, I have been to a lot of places. However I realized in a young age that I belonged by my sister's side. No matter where in the world we were, my true environment was by her side. We love to explore so we would travel to all this cultures and places to find our "right" environment. Honestly, it took us time to find the true atmosphere, I can assure you that, but at least we found it and went for it. By her side, I got to increase my capabilities, where I no longer was neutralized. Her closeness brought up the power within, which is the reason why I need her close. This makes me think of the music video "Wake me up", by the Swedish DJ Avicii (may him rest in peace). In this video, the two girls feel like they do not belong in the society they are living in. This is something the younger girl implies in the middle of the music video when she says "they don't like us", since she felt that they were unwelcomed and that they did not belong in that environment. The older one decides to do something about it and ends up finding the society where they did belong. I find it really hilarious that I was extremely addicted to this song (like many of you I believe). The lyrics spoke right to me, and again, my subconscious knew before my conscious did that I needed to find myself in an environment where I could increase my expertise. But, how could I do this? Well, by firstly, having consciousness of this need. To know that there is something missing in the environment I today live in. And secondly, act. So, what do I want to highlight with this example? – It took them courage and sacrifices to make up their minds and move to the right society, to step into the unknown. But when they found the courage, they ended up achieving far more than they expected: a happier life and the feeling of belonging. If you do not belong in the environment you are currently living in, you need to do something about it. You will need to take small risks and make small sacrifices in order to win big.

Another example I can give is the movie "Latter days", where Aaron – one of the main characters in the movie – is living a life that his family have been setting up for him. He is following his father's footsteps and everything is fine until another person comes into his life. This makes him realise that he is someone else than he thought. He is not heterosexual but homosexual, something the church is against. Aaron could choose to apologize and live a life in facades, but he chose to stand up for whom he was. This leads to Aaron being exiled from the society, since he refuses to apologise for what he is. At the end, he chooses his happiness, which lead to him being in an environment where he got accepted just the way he was, where no excuses of who he was were needed. But, I am not saying that the environment solely make you, do not get me wrong and make sure you hear me. I am simply saying that the environment brings out the different parts in you and if you are in the right environment, that environment will bring out the best in you. Keep this in mind: those parts have been there all along, waiting to be explored. You just need to bring those parts to the conscious from the subconscious. So, here we have two examples on people who acted for their happiness in the end. Now its time for you to do the same!

"Once you say you're going to settle for a second, that's what happens to you in life." —John F. Kennedy

So, what do you need to do if the environment you are living in does not give you joy? You will need to find the right environment for yourself and then spread your wings. If that environment is overseas, then go for it and always think: What is the worst thing that can happen? Is it really worse than how I live today? I mainly focus on that my personality matches the surroundings, and if it does not, I am looking for something new. The reason why is because I have lived a life behind facades, where it took a lot of facing the demons to get out from those facades and roles. Today, when I finally found the real me, I am not letting her get shadowed by those similar roles, facades or masks again. This is the reason why I focus on the surrounding matching my inside – because she is the one I like to keep highlighted. You could see the resembling's with your job. If you are not happy at your current work place, you simply need to look for another job. If you are not happy with your current job, you will get influenced by the environment and start to feel bad, which as a result will destroy your health in the long run – mental wise. Let us take this further. Let us put it in other disputes, shall we? What about the women that stays in unhealthy relationships? Why do they keep staying in a toxic environment when they know it is not good for them? Whenever we see a friend or a closed one go through something similar, we oftentimes advice them to leave the relationship behind and go separate ways. But when it comes to one self, it is something else, is it not? I do not know how many bad excuses I have heard towards people staying with someone who are mistreating them. And I am not solely referring to physical abuse. Fine, you might have shared years or even have children with the person, but what about

53

being a role model for your kids? Is it healthy for them to witness something like that? They will end up growing up in that environment and think that the way you got treated is the right way to behave and act upon. They get influenced mentally whether you like it or not. And worst case scenario – they will use the same abusive actions towards someone else in their life. Remember that implementations work like that. We tend to do exactly like the people in our surrounding and that is the reason why people that witness violence might use it too, simply because that is how they got taught. Furthermore, people in unhealthy relationships will lower their self-respect as a result as well. Why? Because they let someone else continually mistreat them and by not stepping down the foot, they will accept that kind of behaviour against them. And why you might ask again? When you hear something repeatedly, you start to believe that to. That is how powerful the environment is, so if you want to be happy, you need to find the environment that brings out those aspects in you. Do not settle down for plan B, you will be living with that regret for the rest of your life. For a star to be born it needs the right ingredients; for your success to be enlighten you need to do what you are best at in the environment that brings out the best in you.

In the end, you need to make yourself fight for your true calling by believing in your self and your true passion, which goes hand in hand with your self-confidence and self-awareness (this is something we will speak about more in the "behaviour" chapter). Additionally, does it go hand in hand with the environment too, since you need to find the environment that brings out your area of expertise. In the beginning of this section I asked you a questions, namely: *"Are you happy in the society and in the environment you are living in today?"* Now it is time for a follow up question, which is: *"Is the environment bringing out the best in you?"* Being a successful lady, you need to start this journey from an environment that is to your advantage and an atmosphere that brings out the beast in you. And yes, you read right: the beast (it was not a misspell!). This makes me think of Pokémon, where you need to take advantage of your powers and avoid the negativities. Pikachu is one example, where he benefits from water since electricity has an advantage in water. However, Pikachu also avoids areas that are negative for him. So thinking of your life: *What is working for you? Which environment highlights your positive qualities?* Once you have found those areas, stick to them. Then, after finding out what areas that brings out your positive qualities, you need to take advantage of your knowledge and abilities in this location to the fullest. This since you will benefit from them. But – and this in an important but – it can take days, weeks, months or years to find your true environment. The influential facts are within you: your passion of finding what *you* want and what you are meant to do. How badly do you want to find yourself? The hungrier you are in finding you, the faster you will find what you are looking for. And remember, it is not just the society and the people you need to look for, its more *the person within you.*

"Just making the decision to change your life is half the battle,
the other half is to make that change!"

We have been talking about being in the right society and environment, as well as being in your area of expertise. Now it is time to move on to the right mindset, which goes hand in hand with the mentioned section above. But, before diving in to the right mindset, we shall focus on one experiment.

Let's make an experiment. And remember, the example is hypothetical.

You have come to a road where you have two choices in front of you: right or left. But watch carefully because what does this choice of choices, right and left, actually *say*? What do they tell you? What is their story? You do not have a GPS for this experiment so it is no use to pick up your phone. However, as you try to clear the roads, you will see that it symbolizes your future - or two different futures shown by your subconscious. On the right side, you see your family and your current self, where everyone seems happy and peaceful. On the other side, the left one, you see a destination you have never been to before, where strangers light up the picture and your current family is just as a small picture that you have in the background, along with a happy lady that seems to symbolize you. You look at both sides and you do not seem to see any differences at first, except that one of them is a safe card with your family that supports you while the other choice stands for something unknown. When you look more closely though, you start to see that the left image is more bright and you can tell how happy you are, and how much these people care about you, where you seem to have no confusion that your parents are not present daily. However, on the right side you can promptly be able to see that the lady, who is symbolizing you, seems to have some heavy bags under her eyes and you cannot see the glare in her eyes. Again, these two sides and picture as whole are shown by your subconscious. Further, while diving deep into their minds, you find out that your personality in the left seem more of a positive thinker and she also makes sure to live her life from her perspective, always, which also have brought a lot of sadness into her life, since she needed to face a lot of negativities and obstacles to get were she today is. But she fought and won them all in the end, which made it all worth it since she today knows her capabilities and her true potential. The right side, on the other hand, shows a different mindset, where the woman seem to have a "normal" day, where she does her duties to the society and family, but what the others do not see is her dreams: she simply live a life that is OK with her. With other words, this woman does not do anything to achieve her dreams. This woman have some visions and every evening she dreams of a different future and what she wishes for. But when the morning comes, she does her same duties, not doing anything about achieving something else and you sense her absence from her body and dreams, where there is no correlation between her mind and body.

Now the choice suddenly gets better, does it not? For what I am trying to paint up for you is that you must – unfortunately – do sacrifices to reach where you want to be and for some, it means that their family is not going to be around all days. But what they fail to take into consideration is that they will create a new family. Family should be more than blood. It should be more about connection, faith and belief in one another, as well as being there for each other. And by the way, in

58

todays' use of technology, you could always be in touch with your parents, no matter the distance. And by the way, family in this example is a metaphor for your closest ones. So now you might start to understand that if you are trying to make everybody else happy, you might never be happy yourself and trust me, you do not want to be in an environment like that. You *should not* want to be in an environment that has not been chosen by you. And do not get me wrong here. Some people are dreaming of this, where they are in the environment chosen by both themselves and their surroundings, and to them I say: continue ladies, you are achieving your goals and dreams. I simply want to highlight that you need to spread your wings and fly. If you make yourself happy, these people in your surroundings will accept your choices, sooner or later, because they want to be apart of your life. Additionally will you find other people in your new environment that will connect with you in ways you never knew were possible. Unfortunately, not everyone will support your choice but you know what? Everyone who has met you has not all liked you, have they? So do what you want, as long as the choices are made by you – for you. And try to have in mind that it is the path you choose – for you and for your health. Remember that, just because something is on the right side, it does not necessarily mean that it is the right solution for you.

So, my question to you is: which one would you choose, the right or the left choice? Is the path of your life your choice or the environments? And are you the one writing your chapters?

"It is far better for a man to go wrong in freedom than to go right in chains"

—*Thomas H. Huxley.*

PATTERNS, PATTERNS, PATTERNS

Do you, as well as I, have something that drag you down the same old bad patterns again? Do you have something that keeps you from getting where you want to be? If you have answered "yes" to any of these two questions, you have come further in life than those who answered "no". You are honest with yourself, as well as aware of your honest answers, and that is always a great start. The fact is that we all have something that drags us back to square one. An emotion that creates feelings that would not let you move forward. The secret lies in that there are some people that know how to keep walking with that luggage. These people have cracked the code to keep walking, even though they have skeletons in their closet. In fact, there are some skeletons that will take years to eliminate, but as long as you fight to reduce them one by one, at the same time as you move forward, that is when you are further in life than the majority. Simply because you are walking toward getting rid of those skeletons, as well as moving towards success.

WHAT TYPE OF MINDSETS' DO I ADVISE?

The subconscious stands for 90-95% of your mind, which means that your subconscious is the one pulling the strings. Since it answers most of our thoughts, the subconscious mind usually highlights what the conscious mind is thinking. This said, if you are insecure in yourself, your subconscious will work hard towards fulfilling everything that accept that fact. This is something bad, since our bad thoughts will only make us worse. But it is not our subconscious fault. We are simply wired this way. Nevertheless, it is an upside though. Since we can make ourselves feel worse, it also means that we can make ourselves feel better by having positive thoughts. Again, it is all about perception and how you decide to tackle the insecurity. Instead of looking at a downfall as something bad, teach yourself to see it as something that will bring you higher since it is a learning curve for you. Whenever you fail at something, stop and ask yourself why. Usually you have a reason for failing, and when you know, you work harder to redo it. It is all within you, you just need to switch perception. The way you look at problems will determine you. So make sure to have a positive dialog between your conscious and subconscious, as well as your body and mind. That positive dialog will reward you. From the moment you start giving positive fuel, your subconscious will start looking for aspects that support that question, which will lead to you having more positive thoughts, and more positive things will come your way. This is called Reticular Activating System (RAS), which gives you what you search for.

One thing I can advice you to do is to ask yourself: *"What type of thoughts do I need to possess to be able to get where I want to go?"* I ask myself this question every time I feel lost in either the environment or myself. I have a mission ahead of me, but that does not mean that this mission cannot be changed. Sometimes we do things that disturb our pattern, which will either be a learning curve, or something that will turn out to be better. Either way, these occurrences change your pattern. That means, to keep moving toward with your goals, you need to ask yourself this question repeatedly, simply because that is like a map: it helps you where you want to go. But, to fully be able to answer this questions, you need to have the right mindset.

1. VISUALIZATION

If you were to ask me why I visualize, I would answer: "Affirmation helps me get where I want to be. By giving fuel to that vision, I help myself reaching that vision by using my whole body. Since visualizing reaches beyond the conscious mind, you will be able to use all of you." If you were to ask what those visualizations do to me, I would answer: "I visualize two times each days. It is the first thing I do, as well as the last thing I do during the days. I make sure to give a clear view of how I want my future to look like and how I will reach that future. These clear visions and positive detailed affirmations help me get where I want to be by feeding my mental state with the right mentality, everything so I start the day with a strong mind, as well as ending it the same way. However, it is safe to say that visualization and affirmation helps me be more honest with myself, where I become more aware. When I have done something bad, I focus on why I did what I did and how to fix it.

When I think in bad ways, I stop and focus on why I got those bad thoughts in the first place (could be jealousy, hatred etc). On the other hand, when I do something great or I achieved my part goal, I tend to look for patterns so I can do more of those. So to the question what those visualizations do to me, I would say that it helps me get where I want to be by painting a picture and a way to fulfil that picture. But more importantly, it helps me get a more clearer and a more positive picture of myself and what I am capable of. In the end, my visualizations help me to keep myself in direction to where I want to be, as well as keeping myself in the right mindset, with the right mentality."

By visualizing daily, your chances of gaining control over your actions and thoughts are higher. Since you teach yourself how to stay away from negative thinking and focus on all the positivity you want to be surrounded by, you will in return start seeing them. This goes hand in hand with RAS, as I mentioned above. By visualizing it, it will become your reality. This also goes hand in hand with *the law of attraction*, where you get back the energy you put out. By constantly focusing on the positivity's, the energy you will get back is nothing else but that – positive outcome.

Did you know that the human mind does not know the difference between reality and illusion? It is true. This is the reason why people get afraid when they are not in any "real" danger. One example of this might be the ghost houses in amusement parks. In those, we know that we are not in any harm, but why do we still get scared once we are in there? The answer is simple: your subconscious mind does not know the difference between what is reality and what is not, only your conscious does. This is why athletes oftentimes visualize themselves jump higher or longer, run faster, score more goals, win the game etc. – because they know the power their mind holds. This is something we can use to our advantage too, and this is also the reason why we can visualize until those visualizations become reality. By working hard toward fulfilling those dreams by visualizations and positive affirmation, when the day comes, your brain will already think that you have been there before and act the exact way as it thinks you acted the last time (when you in fact was visualizing it all along). That is the power your brain holds. Never forget that. You possess power stronger than anything you imagined and it should also be something you use to your advantage. Whenever you come to a grinding holt, stop and focus on problem-solving. By focusing on solving the problem, instead of wining about it, your mind will help you with all its power to find solutions. And this all happens simply because you put your focus on that. Remember that your mind will help you find answers to the question you ask. Therefore, ask questions that will generate to you finding solutions, rather than questions that will give statements about the negative fact.

Again, thanks to RAS and law of attraction, you will get what you reach for.

2. POSITIVE THINKING

The brain is the part of the body that needs to be kept away from negativity. If you do not believe in yourself or believe in the things you wish for, your brain will be affected by your doubts and as a result, not work hard for it. Why work hard for something it does not believe in? With this said, your communication with your brain cannot and should not be poisonous. If you on the other hand believe in you and a better future for yourself, your brain will believe it too. Dare to believe in it, dare to want it, and dare to work for it. That mindset will grow bigger and bigger and in the end, that mindset will influence you to work towards getting it. Do you see the connection? *You need to make yourself believe in what you want and then you need to fill your mind with positive thoughts to keep yourself fight for it until you reach it.*

What I am trying to say is that the mind is driven by your thoughts and beliefs. You need to study hard in order to pass your driving licence right? –That is your belief regarding working hard towards something. The same goes with visions. The reason why you fail is because you subconsciously do not believe in yourself. Some reasons why you do not succeed with following your dreams might be that you think that your failures will bring shame to your name or that you are not good enough. Either way, those are your beliefs. And this says a lot about your character. Those things I just mentioned are the wrong type of mindset. You should switch that mindset. You should focus on the possibilities instead of the loss, you should focus on the achievements it might give your name instead of the shame – you need to see it as something that increases your character, rather than bringing it down. But this all comes down to one thing: fear. We fear all the loss it might give us. But the same mindset needs to be made regarding fear. Fear is a learned behaviour, where we got this scarcity imprinted in our mind from our environment, as well as different occasions that brought our confidence down. Look back to those downfalls. Try to remember why you acted the way you did, and if you could change that outcome, would you do something differently? It all comes down to how we react to fear or occurrences in general. In other terms, how we manage to conduct a feeling and increase its meaning toward that incident. This can be compared to seeds. If you start fearing something, it will grow. Therefore, try to eliminate all the bad behaviours, thoughts, emotions and feelings in your mind. By switching the bad ones to positive ones, you will slowly kill those seeds with new ones – the better ones, and those positive thoughts, beliefs, emotions and feelings will be the salvation to your future. This said, to be able to reach for what you want, you need to be in alliance with yourself.

You cannot reach success with yourself half-heartedly. To give what I just said a meaning, I would like to give you an example. You tell yourself that your arm is hurting, even though you have not done anything to hurt it. Just to notify, your arm is not actually hurting: what you do is that you actually tell yourself a lie. You begin to tell yourself, every single day, that your arm is hurting, which will result in a period of time that you actually believe that your arm is hurting. Maybe even take it so far that you will need to visit the doctor. This is a result of the communication you fed your mind with. This is the power of visualization and this is the power of communication. You told yourself that it hurts and in the end, your brain believed your words and it also started to act after those words. To take this in controlling and turn it into an advantage instead, what do you think would happen? What would happen if you told yourself: "YOU CAN DO IT!" instead of all the bad words? The result would be you achieving anything you put your mind to. Remember that the brain is the part that controls the rest of the body, which makes this part the most valuable part, which also means that it needs to be taken care of carefully. Therefore, feed it with positive thoughts and you will gain positive actions. Just to be clear, I am not saying that you should lie to your brain. This was just an example to get my point across. This was just an example what positive affirmation and visualization could lead to if you use it for positive outcome.

Smart people underestimate themselves – ignorant people think they are brilliant. [1]

3. BELIEVE IN YOURSELF

There are reasons to why each of us is born. We just got to find those reasons!

CHOOSE THE LIFE **YOU** WANT TO LIVE

Dare to do what you want, not what others want. Remember that you are the one that is supposed to live your life, and therefore should be the one making the decisions for you. Hence, choose your path upon your wishes, not others. Additionally, if you do not see yourself in the society where you are living today, do not feel like you are obligated to do it just because your family, friends and neighbours does it (this is something we have spoken about in the environment-part). Dare to go against the flow. Dare to do what you feel is the right thing for your vision of your future. Always keep one thing in mind: You are the one that needs to be happy with the decisions of your life – you are the one that will live with the regret otherwise. We live in a multi-cultural

---

[1] *It is a cognitive bias called the Dunning-Kruger effect, where the highly skilled assume that things they find easy are also easy for others, and the unskilled are so incompetent that they cannot recognize their own stupidity.*

world, where – if a culture does not match your standards and beliefs – your choices and living standards can be matched with other environments. But you must dare to make the decisions based on your expectations of your life and what feels right for you. That is what a true successful lady does: she is interdependent with herself and dare to make the decisions in her life. This may take time, as I mentioned earlier on, but if you stick with your thoughts, you will make the right decision based on *your* wishes and *your* requirements. Also, keep in mind that if you do not know if this is the right decision for you or not, subconsciously you already know. How? Because if it was the right decision, you would not have to reconsider it at all. You would already know.

There is a sentence that has been imprinted in my brain since the first time I heard it. Oprah mentioned in an interview with Gary Zukav that *"If you do not like what you do right now, that is amazing information for you since it means that you are one step closer to knowing what is meant for you"*. I can nothing but advice you to take this assistance into consideration and realize that if you do not like something in your current state, change it. For example, do something different again and again and again, and in the end, you will find what you like. As a result, you will live a happier life. Me for example, I got this amazing opportunity to work for one of the best firms in the world in that expertise, where I thought that this job would be the start of something great. But, I did not match in that environment or society so I dared to take the unfamiliar path instead of staying there. I was not happy in neither that environment nor that society (it neutralized me and I wanted to bloom), so I needed to do something about it. I took my happiness over money and I took me over résumé. This led to changes in my choice of society and work-path completely. Thanks to that decision, today I am doing what I love – I help people who are in a similar position where I have been. I give back and there is nothing that could make me happier. I have been there and I have master it. Now I make sure to help future successful ladies to ease their path towards their success. However, I am afraid that some people might give up before they even try. I fear that they are too afraid of what the surrounding will say, and therefore give up before they even try. I am afraid that some of you are too afraid of what the people in your surrounding will say if you do fail. This means that you are stopped by the words of others, and therefore acting after those fears and "if only". I fear because I have been there. But what does this say about us? What does it say about a person that is too afraid to follow her dreams? And more importantly, what does this say about our surroundings? Let us change view for a moment, shall we? We do associate the people who follow their visions as role models, right? We tend to admire people that did go for what they wished for, and did do what they pleased. So why do we not do as the ones we admire? What makes them different from us? –It is not

71

what makes them different, but their dedication to put their dreams into actions. They fought for what they wanted, which made them reach for the stars. They too probably had people who would talk if they failed, saying that they would not make it, that they were just throwing away money and time, and maybe even mentioning something like "that life was not meant for them". But these people had the right mindset, which also rewarded them in the end. People who stand up for themselves get rewarded sooner or later, and no matter when, eventually they will. But if you do not take this change or opportunity, you will go through your life thinking about what if. Do you really want that? Would you risk your whole future with "what if" just because the fear of failure and criticism is lurking around in the darkness? I only have one thing to say to that: you need self-efficacy and self-confidence to succeed. That is how I made it through. No matter how much you fail, you will hang in there until you reach your goal. This is what self-efficacy and self-confidence is all about: believing in yourself and your ability. No matter how much the world is pushing you down, always be in alliance with your mind. Because yes, you will have obstacles and times when you just want to give up, and yes, your environment will try to drag you down. But eventually these obstacles will fade away and you will be standing on the top as a successful lady.

FIGHT FOR WHAT YOU WANT

There is nothing you cannot achieve as long as you fight for it. This goes hand in hand with you controlling your action toward what you want. Some people oftentimes wish for a better life in the evening, ending up doing the same thing the next evening. With this said, you cannot achieve only by wishes. What you need to do is to take those wishes into action and only then will you accomplish what you wished for the night before. To give an example, it would be as having a dream profession. If your dream is to become a doctor, then you have to make this dream a goal in order for it to be achievable. Only by working toward your dreams, only by actions, will you be standing as a successful lady in the end. Make no mistake of it, visualization is important, as well as planning, where these two will lead you to both having the right mindset as well as a plan to get where you want to be. But without working towards those dreams, you would not achieve them. That is the reason why actions speaks louder than anything else: simply because that shows that you are serious with these visions. It shows how strong your desire is. Additionally is both persistence and long-term thinking needed, where you would not be able to fulfil your dreams after solely one day of fighting for your happiness. It requires time and effort in a long time of period. The main thing is that you fight for your wants, and will in turn reach it – sooner or later. Focus on you and not how fast the others achieve their wants – that will only rub your focus. There is a reason why Apple always win over their competitors and have competitive advantage, even though their products are much more expensive than the other brands in the same market. The reason is because Apple focus on what they can do *better* or what they can do to improve themselves, whereas the competitors focus on Apple. You see the difference? Apple focuses on their growth, while the others focus on other's business. This is exactly why people who mind their own business will be more successful and happier than the others who only focus on what everybody else is doing.

MAKE YOURSELF BELIEVE IN IT

You need to believe in yourself and what you want as a reality. This is done by thinking in other directions, and therefore acting in that direction. You need to have a positive mindset toward your abilities, and yourself in general. You need to wake up every morning and make yourself *see* the future you want, and then get up and work hard toward that vision becoming a reality. Every night, when you lay in your bed, you need to think about the future you want for yourself and then ask yourself what you have done during the day to get a step closer to that dream. Jim Carrey is a big example of this, where he visualized about the things he wanted, and then worked hard towards achieving them. He said: "I would visualize things coming to me. Visualization works if you work hard. That's the thing. You can't just visualize and go eat a sandwich", which is something I could not say better myself since this is exactly want I want you to understand: to know that belief in you is the best and first seed to your success. But this only if you believe in *yourself.* If you do not, why do you expect others to? My personal experience is that people oftentimes focus on other peoples' thoughts and beliefs about them. Usually do they not allow themselves to believe in what they can achieve until they get acceptance from others. To me, the belief in me is enough and that is the mentality you should strive for. But this mentality is learned. I used to seek acceptance from others and if they did not give me clearance to keep going, I stopped. Later on I achieved self-awareness, self-value, self-belief, and self-respect, and that was when I managed to focus on what I believed in, without their acceptance. When others see your belief in yourself, they will start to admire you for it, and that is also when they fully believe in you. That is one of the reasons why my sister got respected in her amount, simply because she focused on her self-value, self-belief and self-respect. As the TSL-organization always prays, it all starts with you. We are here as a helping hand for one another, as a true interdependent organization should.

If you want a better future for yourself, you need to change your daily routines and you need to start those new routines today, as in yesterday. By only changing your mindset into thinking positive thoughts, your view of the world will be completely different. As I will mention further on in this book, you need to look into the mirror and speak to your reflection. Me speaking to myself, while looking at my reflection in the mirror, was what kept me afloat; what connected my visualizations with me. This "talking to my reflection" made my visualizations more real, which led to me taking them more seriously. You need to speak out loud to yourself and mention what you shall achieve today. That is: you need to put up a today's goal towards the main goal. Then you shall pass the day doing your duties, as well as completing this mission. When you are in your bed in the evening, you shall look back to the goal you had for today and see if you achieved it. By achieving milestones each day, you will be one step closer to the main goal and will eventually achieve that goal with greatness, knowing that you did all that you could. By dedicating something each day, you would be one step closer towards accomplishing that goal. Take the steps of this book-cover as an example, where you need to align yourself with step one before aiming for the next. And now you might ask yourself: What could I do to keep track of my achievements? – My answer to that question is what I usually do. I write a diary every evening. I advice you to do the same. You could focus on answering some questions you have for yourself. The questions could be something like: "Have I done anything today to achieve my goal/goals?", "Have I done anything nice for others?", "Am I happy with myself today?" "What was good with this day and what can be improved?" So, one thing you need is motivation: motivation to get yourself into thinking in these terms, as well as motivation towards doing what is best for you. Most importantly, motivation to take the first step and change your routines.

76

A great example is when you are doing something nice for others. It could be something as small as helping an older lady or a gentleman across the road. This small action from your side will light up their world and her or his happiness will reflect back on you. It all starts with your generosity and will end up with you having a more positive view of yourself and the action you just made. It will also end up with repeating that action since it gave both the opponent and you positive feelings. While we are on it, let us take another example: smile. A person's smile is proven to be contagious thanks to mirror neuron. So why hold in a smile? That would do neither you nor the environment any good. What if a person is having a bad day and reflects upon your smile? That might just make their day slightly better. And believe me, even though the person is having one of the worst days of her or his life, your smile will make the other party smile as well. As a result, you feel happy because your smile was responded. Here is a quote for you to keep aiming for your dreams:

"If your reality begins with your dreams, your dreams will become your reality".

WHAT CAN YOU OFFER THE WORLD?

Find an area of proficiency, not being medium on many. The hedgehog concept can be taken as an example here, where the fox is good at many things but will never be able to win over the hedgehog. Why? Because the hedgehog is an expert at one thing: protecting himself against danger. It does not matter if the fox has a thousand skills towards attacking, the hedgehog will always be protected and is therefore always the victor in that fight. Be more like the hedgehog and less like the fox. We want to be great at one thing since that will give us an advantage in our specific area.

What is your special gift? What is your desire? And what are you good at? These questions need to be taken into consideration for you to be able to reach for success. By following and act after what I have to say in the "behaviour"-chapter, you will be dealing with your *self*, as well as being able to find your true calling. This since you will find your true gift after getting to know your inner self. The environment is an influential aspect too, so make sure to reconsider the environment. This ties us back to the beginning of this chapter with the question: *Are you in the right environment?* Your true calling is the special thing you fight for, never end believing in, and is the thing you have an advantage in. The advantage I had was my ability to find my inner strength towards my self-respect. Why is this a hedgehog and not a fox you might ask? By getting to know me, I will be able to stay in alliance with my self by knowing my strengths and weaknesses. No matter how much the environment might throw itself at me, I will be able to stay safe in my skin and with my acknowledgements. This alliance made me fulfil my dreams by helping women like you to become the successful lady you wish to be. But, to get the glory, you first need to be able to fight for it: you need to be able to work towards achieving your dreams like a maniac and always ask yourself: *How badly do I really want this?*

To make yourself achieve something, you need to know you. However, bad days do exist. I know that we all have bad days, I have them too. The trick lies within knowing yourself. If you know you, you will know that today is not a good day for you to start off the day as you use to. One reason might be that your body does not have its usual behavior. Instead you should focus on something else, such as taking time to do something completely different compared to your "routines", which will give your body time get back to its "normal" state. If you have a bad day, make sure to have some lonely-time, since this will probably relax your mind. Eliminate the entire surrounding and just take deep breaths. It works for me. It is about knowing your capabilities and knowing that you need to relax and find your path back to your normal state. Some of us require a day off, some just an hour or two. We are all different, and what works for me might not work for you. Therefore, make sure to develop your *self* and then behave after what that self requires. Despite, always keep in mind that there is usually a reason why your day did not start as usual. There is something your body is trying to tell you. By taking deep breaths and exclude the surrounding, your body will find ways to get that knowledge into your conscious mind. Make sure to listen to what your body wants you to put your fully focus on.

4. CONTROL YOUR ACTIONS

TAKE CONTROL OVER YOUR BODY BY CONTROLLING YOUR MIND. Every action that you make starts in your brain and therefore, the mind. So, whenever you want to succeed at something, you must put your mind into it and focus on the achievement. Achievements will happen as a result simply because you put your mind into it, and therefore, controlling your body and awareness to act toward that success. You focus on the goal. Since the mind is seeking for answers towards questions you are asking, is it important to understand that you will get what you ask for. This is the power of "the law of attraction", which we have mentioned in the visualization-part. So, as long as you think and act toward a vision, you will achieve it. Therefore, make sure to feed your brain with motivation. Therefore, make sure that the communication between you and your brain is healthier for your today and future, far away from toxicating thoughts and toxicating environments. This makes you the master of both your mind and your body. Napoleon Hill supports this statement by saying: *"We are the Masters of our Fate, the Captains of our Souls, because we have the power to control our thoughts.* We must be willing to control our body and mind, which is one of the receipts toward becoming a successful lady. What do I mean by this? If you are surrounded by negativity, you will poison your brain with negative thoughts, but if you surround yourself with positivity and positive thoughts, there will be no limits to what you can achieve. Further is it shown that people with a positive point of view in life are usually the ones living their life in a better way than the ones with a negative point of view. The reason is because they have a more optimistic point of view, both inside and outside. Additionally are the positive ones better at coping than the negative minded people. Therefore, if something bad happens to you – let us say you fail a course – instead of having these negative thoughts and display the rage towards others (which is a displacement from the negative attitude), try to be positive and see that failure as an obstacle. Yes, you might have failed that course, but you know what? The next time you will asset that course! Keep in mind that you are the only person who can stop yourself. Only you have the privilege to control how you think, what you think, and when you think. Therefore, make sure to see where it all went wrong and change it.

Additionally, keep in mind that you will be in situations where you need to control yourself from making a scene. Make sure to take control of your actions, to be the master of your own thinking and behaviour, which includes controlling your temper as well. Even though this situation or occurrence wants to take out the worst in you, make sure to control your mind and therefore not letting people know by anger how hurt you got by this situation. I know it is hard, but you need to conceal and put the focus on telling them that they stepped over the line – with calmness – which can only be done if you have a dialog with your mind. We will talk more about this in the "behaviour"-chapter, but I thought it was worth mentioning once before briefly. Furthermore, if you have trouble controlling your temper, I have a tip for you: think of something that makes you smile. For me, it is my little brother calling me "Meg[2]" with his sparkling eyes and a smile reaching Venus and back. He got one of those smiles that could make every angry lady smile, which links back to mirror neuron.

By controlling yourself, the act from your side will radiate self-control. This self-control will help you be proactive to the environment instead of being reactive. If you would have screamed and make a scene, you would be reactive to the environment's act. But, in the case where you controlled yourself and gave a calm response, you were in control and therefore the master of your mind. Being the master of your mind will be rewarded in many cases, where proactive people usually are more appreciated than the reactive ones. To give you an example, let us borrow the example from the book "The 7 habits of highly effective people", which was written by Stephen Covey. Let us say that the weather is rainy. If you would be a reactive person, you would completely complaint about the weather. But if you instead work

---

[2] *Meg is a character in the series "Family Guy".*

toward being a proactive person, you make sure to put your energy on aspects were you actually can make a change. In this example it would be changing clothes and choose the outfit after the weather. This is also the reason why the proactive ones are more preferable: they choose to put energy on things they can accomplish and change, rather than complaint or live after the environments' decisions. You see the difference? The proactive people tend to change the aspects they can have a say in, whereas reactive people tend to just go with the flow, where they think that they do not have a say in their live and therefore, their life just "happens to them". So, to take control over your body, you need to be able to control your mind.

EVERYONE MAKES MISTAKES.

We are humans, and humans make mistakes. This said, you need to be willing to learn from your mistakes and not repeat the same misstep again. We are all worth a second chance, but there are no two second chances in a row. Meaning: you need to know what you did wrong and not repeat the same mistake. For example, when you start working at a corporation, you will make mistakes. But you need to not repeat the same mistake again and learn from the mistake you just made. Also, you need to accept that you made the mistake, and not put the blame on someone else. With other words, you cannot run from your fault: you need to face it and therefore, take responsibility. Taking responsibility for your mistakes says a lot about your character as well: it says that you are confident enough to take accountability for your mistakes and are therefore ready to do whatever it takes to redo the mistake you made. And as a future successful lady you should start with accepting mistakes and learn from them to be able to increase as a person, as well as a character.

"Only those who are asleep make no mistakes." – Ingvar Kamprad
(May him rest in peace)

DARE TO TAKE RISKS AND MAKE SMALL SACRIFICES

"To be free, to be happy and fruitful, can only be attained through sacrifice of many common but overestimated things". – Robert Henri.

For an individual to win big, she needs to make small sacrifices, which Robert Henri also implies in the quote above. There are risks in everything you do. When you drive a car, an accident is one of the risks, even though we might not be the one causing the accident. How come people drive cars every day and jeopardies their future by driving proudly, but whenever it comes to making sacrifices for a life they want, most of us do not even bear the thought to go against the society or our parents' wishes? These conditions – to not dare to go against the society or break traditions – are learned conditions, which we make by operational condition. Operant condition indicates that if we are rewarded by certain behaviour, the probability for us to repeat that

84

behaviour is high. But – on the other hand – when we get punished for certain behaviour, we tend to avoid the same behaviour. We tend to avoid anything that is considered a "danger" to us since humans are implemented to move away from danger. This could also be a reason towards why people, who get punished by following their dream, tend to give up and choose the safe road instead of trying again after that fall. Another respond to a failure is by learning from it, which I stand for. This is a change in your perceptions. To see it as an experience, rather than a failure. However, even if some of us know that sacrifices needs to be made, not many of us actually do know that many of these "sacrifices" are overrated. There is a risk in everything we do, but how badly do you want it? If you want it as badly as I did, you realize that the rewards are worth the sacrifices altogether, and that is how a successful lady should think. She should focus on the goal, while even walking through fire. No obstacle is too big. She walks through them all and never gives up.

You need to find your path and develop strength from that road and this thru mistakes, and to never think for a second to settle down for your plan B. Never think for a second that what I did was easy. Yes, I stood up for myself, but I also went against my cultures and the traditions, but my sister and my family supported me so I had the best support anyone could ever wish for. Although I was also aware of the fact that I could never avoid danger, this since you face it even when you step into a car, which was mentioned as an example above. Let us stick with that example, shall we? Even though you knew that your risk of death would increase with 20 precent, but you could get to the place 50 precent faster – and having a 50 precent chance of higher probability of being happy – would you do it? Of course you would! In that scenario, it almost seems like a "no brainer", right? So why do people not take risks in life for a better one, instead of settling down with what they think is the life for them, only dreaming of "what if?" I decided to face my future by writing this book and developing a career with what I am passionate about, but I did not run into it. I let my development take time. I let my knowledge increase and when I felt ready, I went for it. See, to take risks does not necessarily mean that you cannot play it safe; it simply means that you do what feels best for you, in your own ways and in your own time horizon.

"You need to remember that your biggest enemy is you!"

A notification: You need to be willing to sacrifice time to be able to follow your success. Success is something you continuously work toward, which also means that it requires time. Whether you want to be the best version of you, do a career, or maybe you want to be the next Serena Williams, you need to dedicate your mind, soul, and body into it. This also includes time. With this said, you need to be willing to sacrifice some evenings, some weekends, and some social events to fulfil your visions. It is all about how much you really want it. Therefore, an important question to ask yourself is: *"How badly do I want it?"* and *"How much time am I willing to give to my success?"* Remember that it is your self-development and you should give it time, effort, mind and soul.

YOU NEED TO BE WILLING TO FAIL IN ORDER TO REACH FOR GREATNESS.

You need to keep focusing on your goal, without being distracted by the obstacles on the road. These obstacles will try to break you down: to make you stay on the ground. Here is the thing: you will fail, but you will also rise as a phoenix thru the ashes, which will in turn make you stronger than before. You will learn from your mistakes and be able to avoid them in the future. You need to change your mindset and start realizing that setbacks only makes you stronger, without them you would not accept the success as much as you will when you overcome hardships on the road. Believe me, the price is worth all the downfalls combined. These downfalls will only make you clearer about certain aspects, which will be avoided the next time. Additionally will these mistakes make you a better competitor and a better person, which will be worth the pain.

"A winning strategy must include losing." – Robert Kiyosaki

Unfortunately, there are many people that start of their careers with big goals and dreams. After being faced with a few obstacles and downfalls, these dreams slowly fade away and end up as a reminder of "what could have been". I do not want to be associated with a person that settle down with her plan B just because I had a few obstacles facing me and neither should you. Therefore, always focus on the goal and never lose that sight, even if the night seemed overwhelmingly long. After the night a new day will always arise. Darkness will always be lit up by the dawn – otherwise you will end up thinking "I wish I ...", "I regret not ...", and "If I only have had ...". This can be connected to what Kahneman had to say regarding failures. We do – as people – get more influenced by our mistakes than our achievements, which means that we have stronger feelings when we lose or fail, than when we win or succeed. This in turn leads to us avoiding any possibilities of failures, which also means that our life will be influenced by our avoidance of any danger, everything so we do not have to deal with those feelings again. With other words, we built up a shelter to avoid any negative emotions. This is also connected to our survival instinct, where we as species tend to move away from danger, rather than towards pleasure. Our brain is, according to Marisa Peer, wired to avoid what's negative or bad for you. If you have failed once, your brain will only remember the negative emotions or that failure and therefore make sure to avoid them in the future.

However, we need to keep in mind that it is better to fail a couple of times and then succeed from those mistakes, than waking up fifty years later regretting the choices of our life. Let me ask you one question: Is it not better to have failed a thousand times in something you really believe in, rather than make it in something that does not even reach up to half of the belief you have for the first mentioned one? Just remember that greatness was not built from people whom made it directly in something they did not even believe in. They failed. Oh boy did they fail. But they believed in it and saw the goals. They visualized and did not stop until they reached the goal they really believed in. They did not settle down for anything less than that. This is related to Banduras concept: self-efficacy. Only by raising from our failures could we be able to achieve our goals. But in order to achieve all our goals we need to have motivation and will. Additionally do you need to dare to hold on to your dreams. So, as Marisa Peer said, we need to make the unknown known and the known unknown, which goes back to us dealing with our self and our mind before we dare to go after our dreams. So what we need to do is to change our perception when it comes to failure. Everything is about how you look at problems: are you more of an optimistic thinker or a pessimistic one? What you should switch your mindset to is thinking of obstacles as something that will make you stronger, rather than something that will eliminate you. As my better half always told me: chose to see things from a positive perspective. When I asked why, she answered: because that is when your brain searches for solutions towards the obstacles on the road. Never see them as problems, she kept telling me, because that is when your mind will look for anything that supports it being a problem. And you know what happens then she kept telling me. And of course I knew. By choosing the wrong perspective – the negative one – your brain will be limited and only see the problem and therefore be unable to find solutions. By changing view of something as simple as obstacles, you will start working hard toward fulfilling those goals you have. I knew all this. It was the same obstacles, but different mindset. This is what I choose to follow. I choose to switch mindset completely, to change perception toward the optimistic one – toward the one that will help my visualizations becoming a reality. A lady always goes after what she wants, and remember:

Perspective matter – some see what they want in their lives, while others see the things in forms of obstacles that prevents them from getting what they wish. So if you start seeing thru the things that prevent you from getting that, and focus on only seeing them as obstacles, you will tackle and overcome them all. That is the perspective you should have.

So in the end, you need to be willing to make mistakes and fail to have the possibility to stay in the finish line as a winner. How do you think

Mohammed Ali and Serena Williams did it? Do you think they won from the beginning and became role models without failures? – No, it was those mistakes that made these two people icons for many children across the world. They knew that they just needed to get back up. They knew, and they just acted upon those emotions. Muhammad Ali fought for himself. He saw himself as a winner and as a Champion before the rest of the world did. He visualized himself as a victor and fought until he fulfilled that vision, making everyone else see what he had been seeing in himself all along. The same goes for our female icon: Serena Williams, and that is how you as a true successful lady also should think. I do, my better half does, now its time for you to start visualize too. Another role model is Oprah. Do you think she became a successful lady without any setbacks?

Regret the things you did, rather than regretting the things you didn't do![3]

To stand in the end as a winner, you need to be able to allow yourself to make mistakes and learn from them. It is oftentimes the people who have failed and learned from those mistakes and setbacks that win big in the end. Do you not think that they had moments in their lives when

---

[3] *A part from the famous quote by Mark Twain: "Twenty years from now, you will be more disappointed by the things you didn't do than by the ones you did do. So throw yourself off the bowlines. Sail away from the safe harbour. Catch the trade winds in your sails. Explore. Dream. Discover".*

they just wanted to give up? But they did not, did they? They kept on fighting because the fear of giving up was far stronger than any setback they faced. So my question for you is: *How do you react to obstacles? How did you react on the last obstacle you faced?* Me for example, I faced big obstacles – both from my self and from the environment during my first twenty years – where the pressure came from all sources possible. But during my twenties, I managed to get a hold on me. I managed to look within, to find who I really was underneath all those facades and roles I have build up in a period of twenty years. Even though I tried to find the real me from an age of thirteen, at the age of twenty-two to the age of twenty-five, I finally succeeded with this mission. Even though I had failed with staying in line with my beliefs and wants before, in my twenties I finally succeeded. Looking back to those years, I agree on them being my worst, as well as being my best. I got to see my true potential. I got to see my true character: that I got up and did whatever it took to make it through the finish line. I fought for my rights and made myself see what my sister has been seeing all along: that fire and true spirit within me. I got to know *me*, and while I did that, I also could see which people in the surrounding that wanted what was best for me. During this personal development, I also knew that – even though I fell from the horse – I always had the capacity to get back up and this is what made me the one I today am. You will always face obstacles, but it is *how* you react to those obstacles, and *what* you do to those obstacles that will form *you*. Always remember: I

92

knew my capacity, so I made myself get back up! It is all in you head, always remember that. Therefore, make yourself see what you are capable of, and then act towards it. Start seeing differently: start being able to see that giving up is way worse than a thousand setbacks.

> " '*Cause sometimes you feel tired, you feel weak*
> *And when you feel weak you feel like you want to just give up*
> *But you gotta search within you, you gotta find that inner strength*
> *And just pull that sh*t out of you and get that motivation to not give up*
> *And not be a quitter, no matter how bad you want to just fall flat on your face*
> *and collapse*" – Til I collapse, Eminem.

To keep making my point, I want you too read the next quote carefully and to interpret it sensibly. Make sure to understand the full potential in making mistakes, and keep aiming for greatness, crushing the obstacles.

We learn by making mistakes. So try and try and try til' you finally succeed. That is what life is all about. By trying until you reach success, you will ultimately show ambition, motivation and stamina toward all the obstacles that are facing you. Without them, you would not learn how to avoid them in the future, and therefore, never be as thankful for the success as you would by putting in hard work, passion and fuel. For you need to know one thing: if you do not learn how to face and overcome obstacles, the environment will pull you down. But, if you have taught yourself how to avoid them in the future – and win all the difficulties by having the right mindset – you will learn by making the mistakes once, and therefore, be the successful lady you were destined to be, without something pulling you back. So keep aiming at your future, the downfalls will only make you stronger once you get back up again!

ELIMINATE "MANANA, MANANA"

Procrastination is probably one of the worst things a human being use every single day. Whether it is the dishes, cleaning, studies or work. We simply want to do the things we do not prefer "later", and put our time at whatever we consider as "the funny things" now. Your procrastination needs to be erased simply because it is one aspect that will keep you from acting towards fulfilling your dreams. By constantly thinking to wait until tomorrow to deal with it, you will keep pushing it forward and that will become your life – a life filled will "manana, manana's[4]". This will also result in you missing out on things and for what? Because you decided to do it "tomorrow"? I dislike myself for procrastinate some of the things in my younger days, which is nothing I can do something about today. I wanted to loose weight but never seemed to find the "right day", so I ended up procrastinating my "right moment". The reason why I procrastinated was because I had painted it

---

[4] *Manana: "the indefinite future". It is a word that is used whenever someone procrastinate something.*

to be a hard process, which my mind stood against. Since we do not prefer complicated things, we tend to avoid fulfilling them in the first place. I only tackled the procrastination when I knew that there would never be the perfect day and that I needed to do something today to be able to get the body that I wanted to have. Additionally could I only tackle it by switching mindset about loosing weight. I started to paint up a more clear view regarding weight loss. Only by having a less complicated aim towards weight loss did I actually fulfil this mission, which by the way is the body that I continuously and daily work hard to keep. Thanks to the switch of mindset and elimination of manana, mananas. And since I cannot do anything about my earlier procrastinations, I can help you with your procrastination instead. In fact, I will help you with your procrastination right this second. So get out of that comfortable sofa of yours and do something about your future today. To be able to get to tomorrow, you need to face today and why not face this day with accomplishment of tackling down procrastination and making today the start of something new – the start of your tomorrow? Never wait for the right moment, there is no such thing. However there is right now and make sure to make today the right moment to start.

Nobody got successful by doing it tomorrow, they all did what they could today and when tomorrow came – they became someone and went somewhere.

Let's make an experiment!

I want you to look at yourself in the mirror every morning before starting your hectic day. As you look at yourself in the mirror, I also want you to ask the lady in the mirror if she is happy with her choices in life so far. What will her answer be? While you are answering this question truthfully, also make sure to see your reaction, and what your eyes, facial and bodily expressions really tell you.

A reminder: if you have too many "bad days" in a row, it simply means that you are missing something in your daily life – but it may also be just a small adjustment that needs to be done. It is just that, you have to take initiatives against it by admitting to yourself that something is either missing or an adjustment needs to be done. After being truthful towards the lady in the mirror with your thoughts regarding the question, you need to find solutions and start acting toward fulfilling the change you need to do in order to get your happiness back. Start seeing the solutions to the problems instead of focusing on the problems – it is all in how you tackle the situation with your mindset. But I do not have to tell you these things anymore, do I?

However, changes do not come over a night so make sure to stick to this experiment for a longer period of time and you will see you for what you are, and being able to give the things you need to yourself as well. Me for example, I still do this exercise and I will never stop since this exercise is one of the aspects that keep my mentality where it is.

The point with this exercise is for you to see your own patterns. If you do this every morning, you will start to see patterns in your behaviors and actions, as well as your thoughts. These observations will lead to you being able to eliminate the bad and strengthen the good (thoughts, behaviors, actions and communication). You will also be able to realize what you truly want for the lady in the mirror, and more importantly, what you do not want for her. You will also be able to set up ways to escape the "don'ts" and work toward the "wants". These patterns will not be shown in the beginning. This can be seen in any sport and aspect you put your focus on as well. If you, for example, start on a diet with the goal to loose weight, you will not see your weight-loss after some days, will you? That is almost impossible. Instead, it usually takes a lot of days, filled with effort and energy, as well as the right mentality. But during the process, you will begin to see the changes gradually and in the end, you will see the gain more properly. So, if you constantly make yourself think about what you did yesterday to reach for your dreams, you will eventually put more and more time into it and therefore be able to do more with less time. The reason is because you love the changes, not to mention not having to prepare as much as you did the day before. You just act toward fulfillment of your desires, as well as your focus towards your dreams.

THINK FOR A MOMENT: WHAT IS REALLY THE DIFFERENCE BETWEEN YOUR MIND TODAY AND YOUR MIND WHEN YOU WERE A CHILD?

When you are a child, the whole world is yours, but when you grow up, your plans for the future seems to get smaller and your dreams are not as wild as when you were a child. How is that? Why do you not have the same dreams about your future as you did when you were a child? Is it because you have people in your environment telling you this and that, things that eventually make you believe that you have *too* big dreams for yourself? Or is it because the dreams you had as a child are not meant for you? Either way, I have one thing to say to you lady: you have to look deep inside yourself and find that child again – that child that believed in you because if you do not believe in you, how will you expect others too?

Take Elon Musk as an example. Who would have ever thought of sending an electric car into the space just to see how material adapts and work in space? It all stars with a thought, a dream that becomes a goal and then a vision, which will be reached by a mission. But remember, a goal needs to be SMART in order to be reachable. Smart stands for specific, measurable, achievable, relevant and time-bounded. Which means that the goal cannot be too aggressive or unrealistic in any way. But my statement stays the same. You do not need to narrow your view of yourself. Just make sure, as Musk did, to *create* so they become measurable. The power lay within you.

Let us move on. When you were a child, you maybe wanted to become a princess, a doctor, an astronaut, and perhaps everything at once. Even if it was "impossible" for us to become all those things at once, the term "impossible" did not exist in our radar – we believed in ourselves. Or at least I know I did. This is proof toward the society – as well as the environment as whole – molds you into making you believe less in yourself by being woken up with the reality of today.

Additionally, how is it that when we were little girls, we failed but we also made sure to re-do it until we did not fail anymore? But now when we are older, we tend to avoid making the same mistake again? If you have made a mistake just because you had lack of information, lack of knowledge, or just because you were not persistent enough, you need to re-do it. Make sure to do it the right way this time. "Gör om, gör rätt" as we say in Sweden. It means: do it again but this time, do it right. Make sure you have the information or knowledge needed, as well as being persistent enough so you avoid jumping into things too fast. Re-do it until success and erase the thoughts of giving up. Never give up because there is one thing you need to bear in mind: we tell our children to get back up after every downfall, we teach them to take the bull by its horns, and we teach them to never give up. How come we avoid listening to our own advices? How come we advise this to our children but do not act by our own words ourselves? Remember: actions do speak louder than words and your child will imitate your responses after making a mistake. If she or he sees you not getting back up again, she or he will do the same thing the next time she or he falls of the horse. With other words, words such as "fear", "failure" and "reckless" will have a bigger impact on them and therefore, as a result, become too scared to take risks since they saw your reaction towards downfalls. However, if you show them that making mistakes is something you need to do in order to succeed – simply a process along the way – you will teach them to control their fear regarding these matters, and words such as "reckless" and "failure" will not be as influential as the first example.

An aspect that probably has the biggest part is that a child has heart in everything they do. If they do not like it, they simply would not do it. Or this is the expression I have gotten whenever I have been in acquaintance with one and from my childhood experiences. They believe in themselves and do the things they love. Your adult life can be the same. Who have said that work needs to be boring? Who said that adulthood needs to be boring? To be able to win big, you need to put your whole body, mind, soul and heart into it. You cannot possibly expect to reach success by not believing in you, or by not dedicate your fully self in to what you do. That is one of the differences between a child and a grown up.

100

Do you want to know what I think? I think that the term "failure" is something that grown ups have created – a word they pushed into their vocabulary – because when I was a child, I hated to lose. I played football and if we lost a game, I could be mad at that loss until the next game to show the opponents that we were the best team. That is how I did when I "failed" – I made sure to perform better the next time I got the chance. I put everything I had into it and succeeded, which you mostly do when you do something wholeheartedly. *But what's the difference with you then and now?* In my opinion, I think the society and the people in our surrounding holds us back by making us "realize" that we should not do anything outside the ordinary, or outside the box. Additionally do I think that we are built this way, to make sure that others do not have the courage to follow their dreams, just because we gave up on ours. Not to forget mentioning the society's requirements of us, which are unreachable expectations that only creates mental illness. I think that their unreachable expectations, their demands and their "logic" reasoning and not thinking outside the box is where words such as "failure", "reckless" and "useless" comes into play. However, I want you to understand that this is my opinion and feel free to have other opinions and thoughts. In fact, call me if you do. I would love to hear your arguments and who knows, maybe get influenced by your ideas and opinions as well. My arguments, however, are like this: when you were a child and was afraid of the monsters underneath your bed, you ran to your parents who protected you from all evil that existed under your bed or in your closet. They never told you that these monsters were not real or that your fear is less valued because they were not real. They also made sure that you overcame your fear by being there for you, so why can we not have someone when we are older who help us overcome the fear of failure? Why do the majority of us not have someone that tells us that, just because the others who tried failed, it does not mean that we will. *"Reach for the sun and land on the biggest star"* is what I say to myself each morning while speaking to my reflection in the mirror. *But why do we not tell other people this?* My opinion, I think it is our selfish mind that plays a big part, where we compete with one another. We refuse to see ourselves as failures and since we gave up our dream, we simply use childish behaviors to not "allow" others to fulfill theirs. However, we need to put our problems aside and think interdependently. That childish behavior is not an act from a true lady. She is too confident in herself and therefore, always tries to help the person next to her. She strongly believes in being a part of someone else's success. Not just that: we need to stop hating and be jealous of others, jealous that they are more successful than us and hating just because of that. I mean, do not disgust but act. If you hate that your cousin is doing better – well, get of that comfortable sofa and start doing something that will take you one step closer to your dreams. It is as simple as that. By doing something, you will achieve something in return, so stop looking at what others are doing and start seeing that you will get it all if you just stop being jealous of people – you need to start focusing on your path and stop looking on what every other person is doing. Look at your self and you will eliminate your negative thoughts as a result too. Remember the example with Apple. They improved because they focused on themselves, while the others focused on them – and therefore did not improve as much.

As you can tell, I believe that we are affected by emotions such as "fear" and "failure" more today than when we were children. The reason is because the terms have gotten a bigger place in our vocabulary, all thanks to our environment and how they taught us to act regarding failures. And that is exactly how the negativity takes over your mind and brain – simply because you give it more space. So my next question for you is: *How much has your mindset and thinking really changed since you were a child?*

INCREASE YOUR RISK TOLERANCE:

One thing to take into consideration when it comes to eliminating your fears of failure is to increase your risk towards tolerance, something I like to call: risk tolerance. The term "risk tolerance" exists in the finance world, where it basically stands for an investors risk regarding the market. In the finance world, people with high-risk tolerance have learned the power to stomach large swings in the cycle and therefore taught themselves to not panic whenever they face a hard time. This is a great power to possess since they will not be able to sell in the wrong time of the cycle. To take advantage of this term, I decided to include it in this book since it can be a helping hand toward eliminating your fear and frightens. So, what is affecting your risk tolerance? –Well, as everything else, the risk tolerance is affected by the mind. Therefore, to be able to tolerate risks, you need to eliminate the fear that is in your head. And to be able to eliminate the fear that is in your head, you need to get to know what fear is. Fear is something you develop from an occurrence in your past. For example, you got bit by a dog, and therefore avoid circumstances were you can meet a dog. You taught yourself to connect fear with dogs – which is the result of classical conditioning – and this fear will continue to grow until it sucks you in. Just take Little Albert as an example, where the behaviorist John Watson observed the 11 months old boy to prove that fear is a learned behavior and therefore not something we inherent from our parents. He meant that children are born as "tabula rasa"[5] and therefore does the environment have a more powerful impact on us than our genetics. During the experiment, the behaviorist shows little Albert some objects, such as a rat and other fury objects. At first Albert does not get afraid. Next time Watson decided to show the same object, he included a noisy sound. That sound frightened Albert. Watson repeated this act repetitive

---

[5] *Tabula rasa = empty leaf.*

times until Albert learned to not just fear the rat, but all fury white things. Even without the loudly noise. The reason why is because Albert now learned that if he sees anything white and furry, it will lead to an unpleasant sound and that made him fear these objects. And as everything else, if it can grow, it can be eliminated as well. So, to have more risk tolerance, you need to get rid of the aspects that are stopping you, and therefore eliminate the fear you taught yourself to have. You basically have two options here: continue to avoid what makes you uncomfortable, or you get rid of that fear.

If you choose the first mentioned one, to avoid the things that make you feel uncomfortable, you will feel calmness within you. However, you need to know that this calmness only lasts for a small period if time – until you get yourself into a similar occasion. This is the short-term solution, where you will limit yourself from what life has to offer. And what does the TSL-organization think about short-term solutions? The TSL-organization stands for endless development, where we constantly work to develop ourselves to the best version of us, which includes dealing with our fears as well. We deal with our fear so that we can pursue our visions and dreams completely unattached to any fear or phobia. And by continuously working with yourself, you will sooner or later get rid of the aspects that limit you from doing what you love, and as a result, cherish life to the fullest: called personal development.

Additionally will the short-term solution make you more limited each time, where your brain will confirm that this occurrences are not good for you and your fear will increase to more and more occurrences and will as a fire, spread until it sucks you with it. However, I want you to know that it takes a lot more time to eliminate a fear than gaining one, so bear with it. Let it take time and make sure to give it your fully attention and energy to eliminate it, step by step.

If you, on the other hand, choose to do something about it, you will eliminate the fear step by step. By controlling the fear, you choose to focus on what happens within you and therefore attract the resources you need from yourself to get through this, and as a result, also dare to take risks. This also means that you start to be proactive instead of react to what the environment throws at you. But, how do I advice you to tackle the fear? I would advice you to continuously stretch the boundaries of your fear. Think of it as a hair tie, where it can stretch the more you drag it. This stretch will limit the fear you have taught yourself to feel whenever you failed the first time, and that fear you grown in you. At first, you will get scared and maybe even pull yourself out from it because you do not have confidence in your abilities. It is unfamiliar ground to you and your mind does not like it at all and therefore pull itself back to familiar ground. This is why you need to look deeper within you and find that inner strength: that strength that will make you work for it, simply because a life in chains is far worse

106

than a life with freedom[6]. So, what you need to bear in mind is that your brain is wired to avoid fear so if you connect that failure to fear, you will avoid what life has to offer. If you on the other hand change the perspective and use that failure to increase your knowledge, you will see that fear as something not life threatening and that you have been wrong all along. With a changed perception, you will begin to see that this particular fear was not something life threatening, and that this fear have limit you from the real life and for what? Fear? Fear of what? Fear only gets real when you make yourself believe it is a threat, and if its not, it is just something you need to learn to live with. But to make myself clear here, danger is real, but fear is a choice[7]. Make sure to see the differences within. Additionally, try to understand this: you will fail, and you will fail hard, but you will also – with the right mentality – get back up. That is what a true successful lady does.

A notification: whenever you get scared or feel fear toward something non-life threatening, you can try to change your mindset and think in terms of "God what I love coincidences". The reason you should switch that fear to excitement is because you shall outsmart your brain since fear and excitements produces the same hormones. You can easily use

---

[6] *"It is far better to go wrong in freedom than right in chains!" - Tomas Henry Luxey.*

[7] *"Danger is real, but fear is a choice" is a quote from the movie After Earth.*

this until you no longer need to "lie" to you brain, because when you do not need to "lie" anymore, it means that you are already "cured". So, whenever you face obstacles, see it as something you can learn to control by increasing your knowledge around that matter. Your body acts after your communication to yourself so try to see every obstacle as something to learn from rather than something negative, which will make you act and control the situation.

Unfortunately, the gender affects the risk tolerance as well – and in a negative way for us women. According to an analysis on 7 500 people by Psychological Consultancy Ltd (PCL)[8], women seem to be more "cautious" than men. I took the liberty to Google the word "cautious" and the definition in the Oxford dictionary explained the word as "careful to avoid potential problems or dangers". So this means that women by nature tend to avoid danger. There is no chock there really. Women have always been the ones taking care of the children, and did everything in their power to keep themselves from danger. Since cave time, women have been the ones in care, which is the way our brain is wired: to protect ourselves from harm, women more than men (since men were the ones doing the hunting). This can explain the fact that men tend to use active coping, while women – on the other hand – tend

---

[8] *The analysis was based on people's (both men and women) risk personality, where the result showed that 19 percent of women, compared to 7 percent of men, were found o be wary, as well as 15 percent in contrast to nine percent were prudent.*

to use emotional and avoidance coping. As you see, it is all in our programming from our cave time to keep us safe, so what you need to do is to change your perception and make yourself see that it will be an experience rather than a risk. Again: it is all in your head. If you see it as fear, your brain will signal to the body to escape. But if you switch that mindset, your body will not see it as something life threatening and therefore not give the signal to escape. As Marisa Peer says: make the unknown known and the known unknown. I have come to realize something during my development towards a successful lady and that is: everything starts with the brain and ends with the decisions in the brain. Make sure to force yourself into thinking in other terms and paths, which will result into completely different thoughts and behaviors. This will give you more options. I always make sure to base my decisions on terms that will be effective on me, as well as what I want to be remembered for. Once I manage to get courage from my "talking to myself", I start to act toward my goals, where the risk tolerance will be beyond thought – it will simply be normal to tolerate small risks to win the jackpot.

A true lady focuses on achievements. Life threatening fears is something she can understand having an avoidance and phobia to, but if you have fears such as stage fright or fright of failure, you can easily work hard toward eliminating those. What you also could do is look deep within you to see where this fright came from? What was the occurrence that started this road of fear? Where did you fail to an extent that you never wanted to be in the spotlight again? Were you the child that was shy due to her glasses and overweight? If you were, this could be the reason why you lack confidence on stage, simply because you got mocked at as a child and therefore avoided the spotlight since that meant more pain. With this example given, my point is for you to look deep within to find out the cause to your fear, and when you found it, work hard toward eliminating this fear, step by step. This can be done, believe me. Take it from the thick and insecure girl with glasses.

And now you probably think: *What can I change to get more risk tolerance?* To that question I answer: Calmness and patience is a must, fear and doubt a dust. Calmness is required since you need to keep yourself in one piece, even if everything might seem like it is falling apart. As the market, where the ups and downs are totally influenced by both reasonable and unreasonable manners of forces, will your life be influenced by ups and downs as well. These ups and downs will be influenced by unreasonable and reasonable occasions, which are occurred by your inner self as well as external parts, such as occurrences made by a friend. Do not panic just because something is not going your way. Remember that "what comes up most come down" and therefore "what is down, must come up". Patience is therefore needed because you cannot jump on everything that "sounds good" at the moment. You need to know what you are excellent at and put your effort into that. As fashion, you do not jump into every style, do you? I mean, not all styles are "you", right? Therefore you may do the same thing here. Not every occasion is "you".

To eliminate risk thoughts, it helps having a lot of knowledge regarding different matters. By constantly reading, you will get more knowledge. Knowledge that will make you see a problem from different angles and therefore, tolerate more "risks". This since your increase in knowledge regarding the matter will help you to not see the fear with the same eyes, and this will also give you more risk tolerance towards not jumping into the first best thing that crosses your road. This eliminates, in turn, also the doubts you have because now you have gained different point of view regarding the matter too.

KNOWLEDGE

"The mind that opens to a new idea never comes back to its original size."
– Albert Einstein

To get ahead in the world, knowledge is required. People such as Robert Kiyosaki and Warren Buffett say that a person needs to invest in him- or herself – which I agree with. In my opinion, I think your biggest investment needs to be on yourself and your improvements. Me for example, I like to study as soon as I have any time over, where I either learn something practical or something theoretical, whether it is from books, from the Internet, from people or from occasions. Either way, I just want to learn more because I know that the more you know, the further in life you will get simply because you will have a more widen view and not as narrow as before. And as a result, be rewarded for it. Additionally do I know that if you know more, you can analyze more, and therefore discuss more and see aspects from different angles – angles you probably would not have had if you did not invest in yourself. I always keep in mind that new ideas make me think bigger and bigger. I see my mind as a social network. The more I know, the more connection do I have, and the bigger my network get. This will nothing other than do me good. Moreover, there is a reason why people that do their homework get rewarded. As an example, let us look at Daniel Radcliffe, who played Harry Potter in the Happy Potter series. He knew that Hagrid had a house made of wood, which was something the interviewer completely had forgotten. This in turn made a positive impression on the interviewer and the others in the surrounding as well. It also led to him getting the job since he had read the books and knew about the characters. He did his homework, as well as differentiated himself in a positive way. And you know what? – He got rewarded for it!

I read a lot of books and the reason is because I get influenced in different ways, where some books just strengthen my abilities by supporting what I already know, and other books give me more ideas that can help me in my work since it widens my view. I love my job, which is why I read a lot. I do it simply to increase my knowledge so I can do more for the ladies out there. Napoleon Hill said: *"Men are paid, not merely for what they know, but more particularly for what they do with that which they know"*. So what does this sentence really mean? It simply tells us that you need to know how to use the knowledge that you possess. If you cannot use your information, there is no point in having it. You need to know how to put that information into actions. Let us take me as an example again. I took my graduation and had a lot in my brain, but I did not know what to do with it. In my environment at that time, they wanted me to work in a complete different way than I was programmed into – in a way that my brain was not built to work after. This made me feel like I was a dolphin climbing on trees. I possessed a lot of knowledge, but I did not know how to get that knowledge across the room in the way they wanted me to. This made me realize that this kind of work did not strengthen my abilities; it rather neutralized them, which goes against my thinking and the TSL-organizations too. So I realized that I needed to do something that highlighted my strengths. I needed to stop being the fox and find my hedgehog spirit. This is united with the learning abilities in the "behaviour"-chapter, where I will mention that you should find something that highlights your strengths. So, what I am trying to highlight is that, if you do not work in a certain way, do not push it – change the environment to something that works for you and your mindset rather than neutralize yourself. Exact as in the environmental part: find the environment and the thing that works *for* you, rather than against you.

Just as understanding can replace hatred, education can replace fear.

I decided that both the "behaviour" and "think"-chapter to be in the beginning of this book simply because both your thinking and behaviour are the most important parts. If you do not change your mindset, how do you expect everything to go as you hoped? How would you know yourself without making any adjustments? And how would you know that this is what you want in life if you do not know *you*?

As you see, everything that we do is influenced by our inside. The way we behave, act, talk and walk are all influenced on how we think. With other words, these actions are influenced by our mindset and therefore, the way we think. This makes the brain your most valuable part of the body. The "think"-part is unified with the "behaviour"-chapter, simply because the way we think is influenced by our behaviour and our behaviour is influenced by the way we think. This is also the reason

114

why these two chapters are the biggest ones, merely because your act and talk are all influenced by just that: your inside. This in turn means that we need to take good care of it because it can easily be adversely affected, which leads to negativity. Furthermore is our mind affective on our outside, and by monitoring our inside, we will be able to work from the inside out and get our inside and outside to match each other. It all starts with the inside and ends with the outside, which is the reason why the book is structured this way too. This is exactly like a diet: when you start eating healthier, it will soon be shown in the outside too.

Now we have worked our way thru the "think"-chapter. Give yourself a big hug and a "high five". You have done amazingly good, keeping up with this much information. When thinking about it, you are further in life than most people are. You know that there is something missing in your life – and you are doing something about it. I am so proud of you! And I can sense your feeling happy too, as you are smiling at these words right now. You should feel joy. You should feel happiness. You are amazing. And you are also on your way towards becoming a future successful lady, and that solely is worth millions of kisses. Keep pushing yourself though. You are working toward becoming the best version of you and for your future as a successful lady.

And this is a good way to turn the page and leave the "think"-part, and dig into what the "behaviour"-chapter has to offer.

"Unless you open up and share your emotions, no one can understand what you are going thru. Do not hold your emotions back because that struggle will eat you from within thanks to your feelings. Until you actually put words to those struggles, as well as breath life into that struggle, not until then will people be able to feel what you have felt. Only then will you be able to do something (about it). This is how you avoid collecting hardships and explode like the next supernova."

BEHAVE

"If you do not make your own rules or be the person you want to be – the world will make those decisions for you"

What is the difference between "act" and "behave"? Since we will talk about those two topics in two different chapters, there needs to be a difference, right? – Correct! The "act"-chapter states a special occasion or situation, which may be the difference toward behaviour, which states your actions in general occasions imprinted from your childhood.

Your behaviour is influenced by your childhood and therefore, your learning abilities as well. What you have been through during your childhood is the driving force that will shape your future actions. With other words, occasions and taught behaviours from your youth will be what drive your future actions in similar occasions. Usually, when behaviours are spoken, people talk about actions, where they do not focus on psychical behaviours such as self-confidence, self-awareness and loyalty, just to mention a few. But behaviour is more than that. Your view of yourself and your view of others: your thoughts and beliefs of yourself and others are all programmed from earlier occasions. Anger, sadness, jealousy, and happiness are all feelings you have linked from earlier experiences, and the way you feel in certain circumstances is programmed from before. You have been taught to

118

react in those ways, which also shows that you can change certain behaviours – if you put time, heart and soul into changing them. However, as mentioned before, you can only change something if you know what you are looking for. This said, you can only change your behaviour when you know why you feel the way you feel in certain circumstances. Considering the reality of my personal experiences, people often associate self-confidence with negativity. However, I think self-confidence is a must. How are you going to make it in this world without even having confidence in yourself? Or self-awareness; knowing your capabilities? I would like to start this chapter by speaking about behaviour in general, and then go deeper into both psychical and physical behaviours worth mentioning.

Something to have in mind while reading this chapter is that this part will collide with the previous "think" chapter. The reason towards this collusion is because much of the behaviour you have today is affected by how you think and feel regarding a matter. To be clearer: Your thinking is influenced by your childhood, which will in turn reflect on your behaviour, which is influenced by the environment.

How you think regarding aspects, how you feel regarding facing these aspects, and how you behave while facing these aspects, are all far more precious than any other tool. It is what will give you success in the long run.

Your attitude has a big influence on the surrounding. It does not matter what you wear if you do not know how to behave in it. If you have a nice outfit but do not get the response you like, there is usually incongruence in either your act or behaviour. It may be in how you walk, where the walk can show the surrounding that you are insecure in that type of clothing – simply because you subconsciously give away signals that show uncertainty. But it could also be in your behaviour, since your behaviour tells a lot about the way you grew up, and therefore, your childhood. So, to become a successful lady, you need to know what to do and when to do the things you do. But this requires a lot of training. It requires you to become *self-aware*.

So, what you need to do is to increase your knowledge regarding your *self*: aspects that influence you and aspects that turn you on, as well as which aspects you need to eliminate. This will, in turn, give you the fullest knowledge of yourself. But, be persistent! Getting to know your inner self take a lot of effort and time. Again, long-term forecasts. Although, apart from this do you also need to learn how to behave in a specific environment, as well as highlight your pros and eliminate the

120

cons. But, in order to acknowledge your behaviour, you need to dig deeper into your self and the lady who is reflecting the mirror. Remember, you are not doing this alone. I am there by your side in every step of the road. So, let's continue reading – you and me.

THE SELF

The self is our understanding of ourselves and how our surrounding influences us, as well as our understanding of how we should behave to reach our goals. According to Rogers does a person aim toward maintaining stability in her self-image, as well as the consistency between her self-image and the actual experiences in her surroundings. If the connection between the self-image and the experiences in her surroundings today does not match, stress or anxiety (or maybe both) will be the prio feelings as an outcome. But, to be able to understand what he means, you need to know what self-image is. Self-image is basically how you see yourself. In other words, how you identify yourself. To be able to make changes, you need to change your view of your self, and make that view match your image of yourself. One example of when these two did not match for me was when I failed some courses at the University. Since I have never failed up to that date before, those failures were something that did not fit my image of myself, and therefore something that crashed my ego into pieces.

Everything is about how you want the world to see you, but you have to start with getting to know who you are first!

With this said, we need to focus on the woman in the mirror and start working for *her* wishes. Additionally, in order to fulfil your dreams, we must begin with the psychological part, where we need to develop faith in you, which we will accomplish by enlighten your strengths and your true *self.*

By looking into terms such as self-awareness, self-efficacy and self-esteem, will we focus on how these words can affect your view of your self. Additionally will we focus on behaviours that are needed, as well as those we need to bury. Your behaviours were mold when you grew up, which means that the actions you make today is all affected by how you got taught to behave in certain occasions. Some better than others. My main focus is for you to look deeper within you and find your strengths and lift them up. This will also lead to you developing other behaviours that are more profitable for your success. So, starting of with the "woman in the mirror". *Who is she?* And please, remember that behaviour is learned, which means that it takes time for them to change. Just see it as a pattern – you cannot start in the middle, can you?

Looking glass self is a word created by Charles Horton Cooley, where he defined the term as *"defining our own self according to our beliefs about how we think other people see us*". This makes us form ourselves into the environment and create a character that is in consistent with the location, which also means that we can have different characters, depending on the environment. Facades. Everything just to get accepted by the society. This whole thing is entirely about the constructed norms made by the society. The ones that do not fit into these norms are considered as the outsiders, and since we do not want to be referred to as one, we do everything to fit in. This is also the reason why we are willing to change disguises, just to fit in. This is called roles, and we all have them. You have a different role at work, a different role at home, and a different role when you do sport (or do any kind of hobby). We all dive into the role we know is suitable for the specific occasion. You cannot possibly expect to have same personality at work as you have at home. These two different environments require different personalities from you, which is why you put on a role to fit in. This is similar to theatre. We are playing theatre daily and when you come home, the curtains closes. You could take off that mask or the role you used that day or that occasion, and just be you. But, when you have been playing for so long, do you even know whom you are? With other words, we are reflecting a character we know the opposite part want to work or be surrounded by, which shows that the glass self is based on how we think others sees us. *But, how are you seeing yourself?* Do you even know who you are underneath all those facades when you take the mask off?

Self-awareness is a term that is associated with your own consciousness of both you as an individual and you as a person. It simply means your awareness of your own strengths, weaknesses, emotions, motivations, and so on. So my question to you is: *how much do you really know about your self?* The reason I ask this question is simply because the more aware you are of yourself, the further in life you will get. I ask since staying true to yourself – and not flee or hide your true emotions, beliefs, feelings or thoughts – is where the core power lays. The more you know you, the easier you will have to get to know others too. Supplementary, by knowing your emotions, weaknesses and skills, you will be able to control them too. This could be done by putting more fuel into your skills as well as having positive emotions, which will in turn brighten the negative thoughts gradually. By using your weaknesses as strength, you will be able to control how you look at your weaknesses. By using it to your advantage, instead of letting it use you, you will accomplish self-control. Self-control means (according to Cooley) the skill you have to know how to control your own thoughts, emotions, behaviors, and actions. This means that you will be able to control the way you see yourself too, where you can increase your self-confidence, self-efficacy and self-esteem by monitoring your thoughts. This is something I will explain down below.

Starting off with self-confidence, it simply means to have confidence and belief in yourself. The people with high self-confidence are also the ones that believe in their appearances, as well as their knowledge. These people are the ones that know themselves well enough to be able to stand with their own beliefs, and therefore, also the ones that have high self-control. These are usually the ones that have stability both physically and emotionally, and therefore, usually the ones that take responsibility for their own behaviors. So every time you hear a person say: "Her self-confidence is too big", put your focus on another direction. This person simply does not seem to know the true meaning of the definition. A lady needs to have self-confidence, and the reason is because she knows that she will fulfill her dreams by believing in her self and her capabilities. How will she be able to deal with obstacles without a big confidence in both herself and her capabilities to get through it? Self-efficacy on the other hand is how much you believe in your *ability* to achieve a particular task. Self-efficacy was the thing that kept me afloat during my hard times. I knew my abilities and by keep believing in me and what I was capable of, I never lost sight of where I could get. Even though I can admit that the line sometimes was blurry, I kept fighting for a clearer view. Something to keep in mind is that self-efficacy usually can be mixed with a term called objective ability. When you fail or encounter an obstacle of any kind, some people ultimately tend to think that they are not programmed or built to overcome this specific obstacle and therefore quit. This is the wrong mindset! You need to rethink. Teach yourself to see the difference between not having the belief in yourself and not having the capacity. There is a huge difference so make sure to see it before you end up letting every obstacle take you down. This is something I kept telling myself each time I had doubts about my capabilities. Since I had this knowledge in an early age, I also had a longer time to deal with me whenever I got to doubt my competences. This knowledge in an early age also helped me see that I had more time to prepare a strategy toward breaking the obstacles on the way, a path where I did not get torn by my doubts. With the right learned mentality, I also had more time to prepare and overtake the obstacles along the way instead of getting torn by it, and in the end, I finally got to succeed into knowing the difference and acting accordingly. So yes, I strongly advice you to know the differences, as well as increasing that belief in completing any task you put ahead of you. Therefore, learn your own limits and push them so you increase your self-confidence, which will as a result increase your self-belief and self-esteem.

Self-esteem is about your beliefs in both you and your abilities, which is usually linked to respecting yourself: self-respect. However, it is important to bear in mind that a person with a low self-esteem has a tendency to lower her goals whenever she faces some obstacles and fail. Meanwhile a person with a higher self-esteem fight harder towards achieving her goals. One result to this might be that people with a higher self-esteem look at the problem differently, in comparison to the ones with a lower self-esteem. The first mentioned ones looks positive on setbacks because they view themselves and the world more positively, and therefore, works harder and put more force into overcoming it. Whilst the second ones looks at setbacks negatively because they have a negative view on both themselves and the world, and therefore, work less enthusiastic toward facing that obstacle. Causes that decrease your self-esteem might be obstacles in your current state. Maybe you are not where you want to be, or who you want to be in life? Or maybe you have put on some weight, which have generated in lower self-esteem simply because you think lower of yourself. This is bad since these people tend to give up on themselves by having the mentality: "I am not worth it anyway". *So, which one are you? The one that looks at everything through a glass of negativity, or the other one who refuse to think in negative terms and focus on the positive aspects?*

"A pessimist sees the difficulty *in every opportunity; an optimist sees the* opportunity *in every difficulty".* – Winston Churchill

Self-discipline is linked with self-control. This means that your discipline is influenced on how you control yourself, which in my opinion is understandable. So, before moving on to something else, you need to deal with your "self", as mentioned multiply times before. Additionally is patience needed since discipline and patience will make the wait worth it. This said, you could not expect results after one day. Let us take the diet example again. If you are on a diet, do you expect result after the first day? The answer would probably be no. The truth is, you do not even expect results the first weeks. If you do not do a really hard non-calorie diet, which is something I highly do not recommend since the weight will come back on as soon as you start eating again. My advice is to focus on the long term. Take it step by step, since this is a cure that will lead you to victory long-termly. So take it easy successful lady, victory will come. Just focus on working hard and the time will come. Remember that a child did not learn to walk the first time she or he tried. It required a lot of 'getting up' and persistence. This child never stopped but kept trying every time she or he failed. Therefore, make sure to keep the right mentality, everything so you could keep that discipline up. Always think about your first endurance and stamina: when you fulfilled your first task of learning how to walk. Always remember how many downfalls it took for you to finally succeed.

"You can be the most beautiful person in the world and everybody sees light and rainbows when they look at you, but if you yourself don't know it, all of that doesn't even matter. Every second that you spend on doubting your worth, every moment that you use to criticize yourself; is a second of your life wasted,

is a moment of your life thrown away. It's not like you have forever, so don't
waste any of your seconds, don't throw even one of your moments away"
– C. Joybell C.

Moving on to the last definition, the ideal self. The ideal self is the vision we have of ourselves: the person we wish to become. The ideal self and the self-image can either be congruent or incongruent. Congruence is when the ideal self and the self-image are matching and we are what we always dreamed of. Incongruence, on the other hand is the opposite, when these two concepts mismatch. The ideal self also includes your thoughts of you in a time horizon because those thoughts and beliefs focus on a vision you have of yourself. A mismatch between ideal self and self-image will make it hard for you to reach actualization (which is the last step in Maslow's hierarchy of needs). Self-actualization is basically about being the person you want to be: achieving your dreams with the material and potential you have today. However, when your ideal self changes, your self-actualization changes as well. This goes hand in hand with the identity change that can happen when you are changing your environment in any possible way. As you see, when the self changes, the whole personality changes as well. However, if you do not do anything about changing for the better, you will continue to have a mismatch between your ideal self and your self-image and that will lead to you never reaching self-actualization. This will – in worst-case scenario – result in you not liking the woman in the mirror and therefore turn your focus to the one in your dreams instead: a lady that you could have been. If you settle down with this perception of your self, to love the dream instead of doing something about the reality, then that is exactly what it will remain: a dream. Why not get to know yourself – to actually take action into knowing your truly self – and make that self match your ideal self? By taking this action toward fulfilling that task – to match your self with your ideal self – that moment will be the moment when you reach true actualization. Me for instance, I daydream and visualize a lot about how I want my future to look like, and then I – at the same time – also makes sure to work toward a match between my self today and my self tomorrow. I simply work toward there being congruence between them.

Having read this far, I imagine you are tired of all the definitions you have been reading about. To eliminate this tiredness – and to use those definitions – let us do an exercise together. Close your eyes and take deep breaths. The reason why we close our eyes is because we want you to focus on the answers from within, and eliminate outside forces to interrupt in those answers given in any way. After taking five deep breaths (to relax your mind), start to think about your future and the person you wish to become. What do you dream of achieving? How do you see yourself? Do not be shy; dream away and dig deep to find your rightful answers. Unlock whatever you have inside that matches that

130

answer. When you are ready I want you to open your eyes. *Now we have one thing to do: now we make sure to fulfil the vision you just had.*

THE LEARNING ABILITY

Learning ability is usually associated with how "good" you are at learning things, as well as how fast you learn. Or at least this is the expression I have gotten when I have spoken to people about learning abilities. However, I think this is something worth mentioning since people usually do not talk about their youth and their childhood having something to do with their learning abilities today. People seem to solely put focus on a person "being clever" just because she is good at learning things right now, not even having the knowledge that her learning ability is influenced by her childhood and environment. To a person who knows how to learn things, I would not say clever, I would rather say that her learning ability is better. It has nothing to do with how clever she is: it is more about how smart she is. But, this is my opinion so feel free to disagree. My thoughts regarding the matter are that people misjudge a lot regarding this substance. Me for example, I am good at memorizing things. For example, where in the book I can find a certain thing, as well as memorizing what I see by disputes before I get a hold on what the word to this definition is. But I am not cleverer just because of that. If I am cleverer, that is because I am following my heart and focusing on what I am best at, not because I have a good memory. My opinion is that the clever people are the ones following their hearts and what they are destined to do with their lives, since they are the ones ending up with a happier life by doing what they love. You may be smarter or more intelligent if you have special abilities, but if you do not highlight or put effort into increasing those, you would not be clever, only smarter and more intelligent.

My opinion: people are different and are wired differently, which means that some of us have a more logical thinking, while others have a more analytical skill-set. The third may be more cultural and expressive, while some are more into sports. We are all different so who are we to say that the ones with the best IQ[9] is the smartest? Why not focus on EQ[10] instead? Some of us have a more analytical and observant mindset, where we have the ability to understand people in a complete different level, as well as put ourselves in the opposite persons' shoes. By having the skillset to be able to put yourself in the opponent's shoes, you will also know how these people will react in different circumstances. The people with a high EQ have empathy that is bigger than themselves, where these people tend to focus on helping others. Who am I to tell this specific person that she is neither intelligent nor

---

[9] *Intelligence quotient (IQ) measures a person's intelligence through his/her individual ability's from logic reasoning in comparison to their fellow human beings.*

[10] *Emotional intelligence (EQ) on the other hand measures a person's ability to understand his/her emotions, as well as the emotions of his/her fellow human beings.*

smart just because her IQ is not as high as Einstein's? Who am I to call her out on stupidity words just because her brain happens to *not* be wired into having the mathematical skills of an engineer or astronaut? Who am I to tell her that she is stupid, when in fact, that lady happens to be me?

By looking too much into IQ and exclude all the other Q's, people tend to make assumptions based on one instrument. I dislike categorizing people and that is the reason why I like to focus on a person's positive aspects instead of solely focusing on IQ. I have a great IQ, but my heart lays in EQ and SQ[11]. I am wired that way, which is why I focus on those areas of myself. This is why we need to start seeing a person's strengths in more than one instrument. We have different feelings, different cultures, different religions, different mentality, but we tend to have one type of instrument. That is weird, is it not? As a successful lady, I focus on all the strengths a person possess instead of being influenced or amazed solely by IQ. By digging deeper into your self and getting to know more about you, you will gain a knowledge of your capabilities that is far more precious that one type of instrument. By digging deeper into your childhood and what you learned and highlighted during your youth, you will be able to gain something far better than anything else – you will gain the knowledge of how to

---

[11] *Spiritual intelligence (SQ) forms from your principles, values and beliefs, where you connect yourself to your soul and follow your purpose in life.*

become a hedgehog on your field, and that is what makes you clever!

Something we learn in an early age is to cooperate with one another. When we are children we usually get punished if we say something that was considered bad, rewarded if we have done a great work, and taught to if we have done something the wrong way. This relates to operant conditioning, which is a concept created by B. F. Skinner. According to Skinner, a behavior can either be amplified or extinguished depending on the consequence of the behavior. If we, for example, have lied to our parents, we are most likely to be grounded (punished). If we on the other hand have done all our homework, we tend to be rewarded with dessert or the evening off. This is exactly how the society is built: we are rewarded for our good actions and punished for our bad ones. This is taught in an early age since we need to fit in to the system, and therefore, the society. We need to have manners. This is why we have laws and regulations, to keep people in alliance with them. Without it, it would be a whole mess to say the least.

So, in your youth you learned to cooperate with people, but also other aspects such as math and language. During this time, you also got to know what type of character you have, which usually is shown in your learning abilities. Did you pass you math tests without studying, or were you the person that was more artistic? Did you highlight those abilities or did you let them fade away? The person you are today is affected by how you grew up and those decisions you made back then. This means

134

that the way you think and behave in certain occasions today is affected by your youth, and the people in it, such as teachers, neighbors, parents, siblings and friends. Did these people help you increase in your demanding area, or did they let you fade into neutralization?

As you see, everything you learned during your childhood affects you today. Conversely, is it important to bear in mind that people can change their behavior, which is often done when you move to another environment: you want to fit in. During this change in environment, you will do everything to adjust to the atmosphere and eventually, you will start behaving as the people in that environment – you will gradually change your behaviors so it fits the environment. Additionally do you normally change your behavior when you experience a certain incidence as well, maybe a sickness or a break-up. That grief and that force you put into that experience will make you stronger than you were before simply by focusing on how you feel and how to survive with that loss.

"Learning is a changed behavior that is based on experience" – *Salomon.*

As much as your childhood being a part of your learning abilities, the self is influenced by it as well. The self makes you fight for what you believe, which ultimately opens up your brain for more information. I will give you an example on when I was my own self-destruction. At University I failed a lot the first semester, which broke me into pieces. This also led to me destroying myself by not believing in my capabilities or myself. With other words, my self-belief, self-confidence and self-efficacy where replaced by self-destruction, self-harm and self-doubt. This all comes down to one thing really. Do you know why I failed? – I failed because I did not know what my learning abilities were, and this simply because I had never studied economy before in my life. I did not know how to approach the studying. I was more of a psychological person, which meant that I was wired in a complete different way. Since they are complete different topics, I could not use the same learning approach as I have done before. The problem was that I was unaware of this, which made my University years a lot harder than they could have been. But since I always wanted to have my Masters degree in economy, and since I did not see myself as a quitter, was I left with the awareness that I needed to fulfill what I started. I knew that some adjustments had to be done. With that vision in my mind, I succeeded. My meaning with this example is that we are all different and therefore have different learning abilities. We all have different strengths, as well as the way we come across those learning skills. Some people learn faster, others slower, some people learn by sitting by themselves, other by discussing. You need to find your *self* and *your* learning abilities. Then you must act in line with those learning abilities.

To clarify the topic, I will move on with the story of myself. As I got to know my self and my learning abilities, I also got to know my learning skills. My type of learning was to, first of all, get to know the definition by myself, and then discuss the matter with others, merely so that I could understand others' point of view regarding the topic too. Since I knew that I was more of an analytical person, I knew that I needed to put my thoughts in contrast to others, and by sitting by myself first and then turn to external parts, I fulfilled my type of learning abilities. This was the main reason for my failure during the first semesters – I sat with the others and there was too much talking about other things (my opinion). For me, this method was bad since I preferred to focus on quality-time and this was everything but that. However, this method worked for them since they passed the classes and I did not. So, I am not saying that it is a bad method; I am just saying that it was not the right one for me. Before I found out *why* I failed to the lengths that I did, my setbacks wounded my soul. Subsequently, today I realize how important it is to understand that you cannot learn an elephant to climb trees. Like animals, are we programmed differently and therefore do we need to be taught in different ways. So, until I learned *my way,* I failed and broke my self into pieces, pieces that I slowly glued together when I mastered this knowledge, which made me stronger than ever in this area.

To emphasize the hardship, this road was not easy. I had a lot of self-doubt, self-destruction, self-hatred and self-harm, and lacked self-awareness, self-belief, self-confidence and self-respect. Even though I have had a long period of time (since I was thirteen) to gain that confidence, it all broke down because I poisoned my mind with doubts. This highlights the importance of working with your inner peace every single day because doubts are like drugs. They will lurk in the dark and the more you use it, the more hooked you will become and in the end, it have sucked you into its darkness. I had this knowledge back then too, but it happened so fast. I did not even have time to reflect. I was filled with anxiety for what was about to come, depression for what already had happened and all drown in devastation, not believing in myself. At this time, I knew I wanted a different story for my future, and I had a vision of what future I wanted, but I did not know what to do about my today to get there. I think you can relate to this, can you not? Yes, I have also felt that. I had a vision but I did not know how to tackle this specific obstacle to get there. This is where my better half comes in to play. I have her to highlight for my transformation to the lady I have become. She helped me find a method that worked for my type of thinking and learning. Additionally did we overcome my obstacles by focusing on how my social phobia, anxiety, stress and misophonia[12] affected my learning skills negatively, where she assisted me to see my

---

[12] *Misophonia = a chronic condition where the individual may feel an autonomous excitment when the individual hear some annoying sounds.*

disadvantages and to use them to my advantage instead. This made me pass the tests, which in turn gave me self-confidence, self-efficacy and as a result, my self-image grew stronger. *I grew stronger.* I simply showed my self-efficacy that this is something I can do. I stood up for my *self*. So, my advice to you is: find your way of learning since we are programmed differently, but also make sure to find your strength and give that strength everything you got. I am here to help you. Just lean on me, I will help you get through this.

"You cannot learn a dolphin to live above water, which highlights the importance of knowing yourself and your strengths. Find that strength and aim at making it stronger – our differences make us special so what is "normal" really? It is your job to find your true calling since that calling will make you special in your own way. That specialty will make you a star."

So my guidance to you is: you need to rely on your knowledge and your abilities, and then keep the focus on those parts of you. Get the help you need, since it is hard to face these changes alone. Find a supportive person (the TSL-organization is always here for you) and always bear in mind that you will never be the best at everything you do and that is ok – as long as you are giving fuel to your fire of expertise. It is always better to be the one people listen to when it comes to one area, rather than being the person people does not listen to at all.

WHAT TYPE OF BEHAVIOUR DO WE WANT TO HIGHLIGHT? AND WHICH ONES DO WE WANT TO DARKEN?

By getting to learn more about you, you will be showing more of your true charisma. Charisma refers to your charm, which a lady use to her advantage since she knows the fact that we are all different and should use our differences to our advantage. To take charismatic people into consideration, these people tend to focus on similarities between them and the surrounding, instead of focusing on disagreement topics or what divide their thoughts. The reason why they focus on the similarities is because they want to find something comparable to talk about. Additionally will these similarities bring value to the person you are communicating with, simply because they feel valued. This can be backed by Robert Caldini, who mentions in his book *The influence of persuasion* that a feeling of similarity between two is one of sixth most powerful influences when it comes to persuasion. The reason of its importance lays in the sync two people feel between them. That is the reason why charisma is one of the behaviors we want to highlight. Persistence and enthusiasm are two other, where the term *persistence* means your ongoing actions toward your goal, no matter the obstacles (which is something we mentioned in the "think"-chapter). "Den som väntar på något gott väntar aldrig för länge" is a saying we in Sweden often use and I always have this quote in consideration. The reason why I include this quote is because it basically says that you will reach for

140

greatness, as long as you keep fighting for it. The true translation towards the saying is "The one who is waiting for something good never waits too long". Therefore, *always get up after you fall*: that is my lifelong advice to you.

Persistence merges with both enthusiasm and your fighting spirit. Enthusiasm means having a positive energy about something, which is needed for a lady since positive thoughts generate positive feelings, which in turn leads to positive actions. Passion and discipline are two behaviors that are needed for success as well. Passion is the thing that gives your life energy, energy to keep pushing you towards achievement of a certain goal. Discipline on the other hand means the practice you have on obeying instructions of any kind, even if those instructions comes from yourself.

"The reason why Sun Tzu at the head of 30,000 men beat Ch`u with 200,000 is that the latter were undisciplined" – Sun Tzu.

I found this quote in the book "*Art of war*" by Sun Tzu. This quote highlight the importance of the messages I want to emphasize with this book; things I wanted to bring up so you can understand the importance of aiming with your eyes open. Even thru the storm. This is called being focused on the goal, but also being disciplined by obeying your visions and work toward them. The road will be foggy most of the time so you need courage to keep aiming and fight, even if you do not seem to see clearly.

Until now, we have only spoken about the capacities and behaviors we need to highlight to become a successful lady. But what about the behaviors we need to brighten? Well, considering the circumstances, negative thoughts are something we need to eliminate right this second. We only need positive thoughts; no negativity is welcomed into your brain. The reason for this is because negativity is a poison that will take you into its darkness. You will also have a hard time getting back from that toxicating darkness and those toxicating thoughts that determine you, which is time you cannot afford throw away. Apart from this do you also need to get rid of that thick head of yours. The reason why is because you need to be willing to listen to other peoples' arguments and what they have to say. This means that you will need to be more open for suggestions and widen your view. This will in turn increase your success in the long run. You will also be able to see things from different angles and that should never be considered as a disadvantage. Short-term thinking is correspondingly something that we need to get rid of – and replace it with long-term thinking. Think dieting, where you need to focus on losing 10 kg within 20 weeks to keep the body on that level. Instead of losing that amount in 3 weeks of constant starving, followed by gaining them again, which is a setback for you and your ego. Therefore is your short-term thinking a setback we need to get rid off.

Control is something you need to have of yourself, where losing your temper is something that should never happen. This means that we need to increase your self-control and eliminate the lack of it, even if you are in a situation where you feel like you are being attacked. You still need to maintain in control of your mind and soul. This is where three deep inhales is in order to be in alliance with your mind. We all have been there, where we have been dealt a bad hand as well as us having bad thoughts about a person. There is no shame in that. You just need to be aware of your own thoughts to be able to control them by changing your old patterns of prejudices etc. This is connected to self-control, where a lady aims toward controlling her every nerve, which is something you need to do as well. Another bad habit is stress. Stress develops from a situation we put ourselves in, where the body feels like it requires more than it can give. This as a result will make the body feel threatened by the situation. When I get stressed in my current state I simply make sure to take deep breaths while I ask myself: *How come I got stressed by this? How much time do I have and what is stopping me?* After answering these questions, I usually get the knowledge on why I got stressed in the first place, and usually it is because I need all the things done simultaneously. But, by answering the time-question, I get to analyze how much I need to do and then act by dealing with them one by one. To not let the stress take over you is something that takes time to control. Since stress put us into "fight or flight" position, do we need to have the right mentality to be able to tackle this programing we have from cave time. Thus, by stopping and asking yourself *why you feel the way you feel*, you will be able to explore yourself as much as why certain things stresses you out. Just to notify something, a little pressure is always good for your body. This because the mind sends extra energy to the body in order to fulfill a specific task. The dangerous part is when these occasions are too many or in a longer time of period. That is when this pressure develops to stress. Our bodies can deal with short-term stress. However, long-term stress will only break us since our body will think that we are constantly under attack, and that is when we break our own body from within. This is where the long-term stressed people have taken themselves in today's society. Their bodies think that they are under attack all the time and in the end, their bodies cannot take it any longer. However, it is important to associate your thoughts to the previous sayings, where we talked about the self, and how to increase your belief in you, and therefore will be able to know what to expect from your self, which is one of the reason to follow this book toward success.

"We create stress for ourselves because you feel like you have to do it. You have to. I don't feel that anymore". – Oprah Winfrey

144

Oprah is one of my role models simply because she is an example of a true successful lady. I also agree with her saying above: you do not need to put yourself into positions that will make you choose or run from one thing to another. Make sure to do things you want to do, not things others want you to do. Additionally is it important to have some quality time. Why you might ask? To this question I answer: because it will reduce your stress. The reason why it will reduce stress is because that quality time will be as a recovery and therapy to your mind. Always remember that the more stress you have, the less control of your body and mind you will have. So my advice to you is to think through your "normal" week and see which aspects and incidents that increases your stress and when you find it, you need to reduce it and even eliminate it if possible.

Another behavior you need to eliminate is your request of approval. Some people are too insecure in their own skin that they look for approval from the outside, instead of looking within. As mentioned, these people are uncertain in themselves and are therefore afraid of critiques as well as being left out in the dark. Subconsciously, what they really are afraid of is their loss in themselves. What they should do is find themselves and realize that they themselves are the ones that should be the one they look for approval from. Instead of looking out, they need to look within to find themselves and to find their own importance and worth. By doing this, these people will be able to stand up for themselves, and in the end, look within instead of without. This said, if people find you reliable, but you lack reliance to yourself, it would not matter how many people that believes in your reliability, when in fact, you do not believe in it yourself. So in contrast to approval, it does not matter how many people that put emphasis on complimenting you if you yourself does not compliment yourself in those aspects. That is the reason why your communication with your brain maintains as the most powerful thing – since you have the remote to your future.

THE PHYSICAL ASPECT IN BEHAVIOR

Until this moment, the mental aspects have been dominating the chapter. However, we need to have manners and behaviour in certain ways too, which goes under the physical aspects – and that is what this part of the chapter will focus on. It is time to move on to physical abilities, such as keeping eye contact, a firmly handshake and your punctuality. We have been using our learning skills since we were children, where we learnt how to walk, talk and act in certain ways, only by imitating the people in our surroundings (which is called mirroring or mimicking). Our politeness is something we develop thru our childhood, where the surrounding mostly influences us. So we usually do say 'hi' in the same way as our parents do, since we got that learned from them. This is also where the handshakes and eye contact plays a part. Since the human being is good at adapting to the surrounding, it can be changed. However, I want to highlight that behaviours are not easy to get rid off so you will need time and persistence to change these non-verbal signals to be able to use them to your advantage. This because behaviours in general are learned and sits deep in us and therefore does it take time to break those patterns.

Starting off with the eyes. People usually say that your eyes is the reflection to your soul, and I can agree with that saying simply because your eyes will not tell a lie. Even if you tell people that you are feeling OK, your eyes and the rest of your facial expressions, as well as your body language will tell the truth. I say this from true experience, where I had this friend that had a break-up with her boyfriend. She told everyone that she was feeling fine. However, I saw the sadness in her eyes (that she was trying to hide). I knew that she was telling a lie, which I also confronted her when we were alone one evening. And you know what? She did not hide it. Do you want to know how I was able to see it? By looking at her gestures and what her body told me – not the words that came out from her mouth. Her body was hunched, were the breakup had made her doubt herself and do you know what the body does when you doubt yourself? It hunched for the very reason that it wants to make itself as small as it possibly can get, everything to not take up as much space as they probably would if the same person were confident. You simply see the doubt in a person the way they minimize the space they take. Apart from this was I also able to see it in her eyes, where her usual sparkling eyes did not sparkle at all. Quite the opposite really. They were really tired and if you looked closely, you could also see the dark bags underneath her eyes. Those bags gave away nights of doubts and pondering. I also recognized the change in her voice, where she usually had a higher tone of voice, but these last days she have had a soft and quiet voice, which was also a warning. All and all, by knowing a person's usual behaviour, you could easily tell when they are reacting in a different way. And when they do, you should confront it with help because those differences in their behaviour are doing just that: asking for your help (subconsciously). While focusing on someone's postures, gestures, facial expressions, voice and body language as whole, you will see more than what meet the ear; you will *see* what is actually being said. This means that the non-verbal communication will signal your true feelings. Even if you want to lie and try to hide your true feelings, your body will signal the truth in the end. All this is included in the non-verbal communication, which is something we will talk more about in the "talk"-chapter.

Sticking to eye contact, it is probably one of the key factors to knowing if a person has a strong or a weak personality. This said, by looking into a person's eyes, you are able to see if she is confident in the way she maintains the contact. If she looks away fast, it probably means that she is insecure in one way or another. She could be shy but she could also be insecure in your presence or in this particular situation. Either way, these people are considered to have a weak personality. On the other hand, people that tend to have a strong eye contact are the ones that are considered as strong personalities, simply because they are confident in their own skin and the environment they surround themselves with. Moreover does a person that has higher self-control keep eye contact more than the ones that lack it, which also makes the people that lacks it the ones that usually are associated with lower self-esteem and self-efficacy. It is important to keep eye contact with the person you are communicating with. The reason why is because by keeping eye contact, you make yourself more committed to the conversation and more trustworthy as well, which is why you need to deal with your inner self and change those parts of you that you dislike. Again: inside out. However, you need to remember not to look into a person's eyes for more than four seconds in a row. This could make you seem intimidating. In Sweden we have something called "lagom", which is where I want you to stay when it comes to eye contact. "Lagom" means neither too much nor too little, which is a perfect synonym here. With this said, I do not encourage you to look away. I encourage you to form a triangle between one of their eyes, to the other, and then to the forehead. And then in repeat. This will make the conversation more "natural" for both you and the opponent, where you will not intimidate her or him. This trick is also supported by the Pease-couple. Nevertheless, a shy person does not usually keep eye contact, which is a complete different topic. As a lady, you need to get rid of your shyness, even if you are shy by nature, and the reason is because you need your communication skills to be "A-style". This means improvements in your communications skills, and elimination of any sort of shyness. By dealing with your self, you will be able to find *you* and get rid of your shyness, since it usually is a defence mechanism from an occurrence in your past. I know this to be a fact because I have personal experience regarding this topic. If I could make it thru, so can you. Remember that I am betting on you! Although, I want you to notice that these rules should be obeyed when you are in the Western. If you are in China, Korea, Japan, or Asia in general, it is important to do the opposite. In these nations, you do not look the older people in their eyes. This out of respect. What I want to highlight is to do your homework. When you are in Rome, do as the Romans do, which is something you should live by – to implement yourself in their culture, out of respect. I also want to highlight that most of my advices comes from my perspective, the Western way, since this is the way I grew up.

Your handshake is also something that says a lot about you, which I have been told from my uncles as long as I can remember. The people with firm handshakes are usually the ones with bigger self-esteem, self-efficacy and self-control they kept telling me. The ones that has a

150

handshake that is less firm will be associated with less self-control and therefore not as outwardly as the others. Which one would you have in your company? Even if the second one, the one with less firmed handshake is a better fit, people tend to choose the confident one because they brand themselves better. More importantly: they *know* themselves better. *It is all in how you make the other part feel.* And to know what the other parts wants, you need to know you. That is why your handshake is important so make sure to practise having a great handshake by dealing with your inner self. Last but not least, your punctuality. It is important to have a good punctuality, since it makes you respect the other person's time, as well as organise yourself into greatness.

A negative learned skill though, is our uncertainty in ourselves, as well as our indulgence. One of the big problems in today's society is the laziness and self-doubt. By having home delivery and the whole world in our hand (iPhone or Android), we lazy ourselves into our homes, were we ultimately become more and more stuck since we are "social" on the Internet with a person a mile away rather than the ones in our surroundings. With today's media, fashion and Internet, we also have a hard time with our self-esteem and self-doubt, where the word self-esteem slowly fades away, and the word self-doubt takes its place. We get influenced by social media and start to hate what the reflection shows. The older we are, the more we tend to get influenced by our surroundings, ending up finding "problems" in ourselves – problems we never seem to have seen before. We can even go as far as torturing us to become the "perfect" girl. I call this an illusion. There is no such thing as perfection. We are all human and human makes mistakes. So in a hectic world, we need to find ourselves and make us realize that there is no such thing as being perfect and without failures, we will not be able to succeed.

Another negative learned skill is misuse of authority power. Never – and I repeat never – misuse your knowledge. Even though you have a lot of it, never use it to stamp on a person's feelings. This is strictly forbidden according to our definition of a successful lady. This also goes against what the TSL-organization stands for. People who misuse either their position or their knowledge of certain things might just be insecure in themselves. That insecurity could make them taking it out on you, since this is something they at least know and could have control over. To be more specific: they are not stable in themselves and therefore taking it out on you. Maybe you remind them of a person that they do not have good memory of, or maybe you have something they subconsciously want, who knows. But, if this person is misusing their power more than once, you need to make sure to confront this person. Remember, one time is no time – you can let it slip. But never let them repeat that misuse or let it become a habit of theirs. Misunderstanding, disrespectfulness, disloyalty, lying, misuse of authority power and lack of character are terms connected to people whom I keep myself from. Why you might ask? Simply because these behaviours will either bring you into anxiety which will turn to depression in the long-run, or their behaviour will bring you to hit the rock bottom by other mental illnesses. The reason why they will have that impact on you is because they will slowly take away your self-confidence, self-esteem and self-awareness. This is something we want to built, not torn. Again, the impact and influence of our environment. However, I also want you to bear something in mind. You need to remember that the type of people who do stamp at your feelings are actually just making themselves feel better, solely by hurting others. In some cases this has something to do with the fact that they have been mistreated before. Some of them maybe just want confrontation and attention. In some other cases people just do not know better. That is the way they used to be treated and therefore the way they are treating others. These people are "just" doing as the environment they grew up in had taught them to act. The six behaviours I mentioned above (Misunderstanding, disrespectfulness, disloyalty, lying, misuse of authority power and lack of character) also happens to be the six behaviours I dislike, which is also why the TSL-organization is built on the six aspects;

- **Understanding** in yourself and others,
- **Respectfulness** for yourself and others,

- **Loyalty** towards yourself and others,

- **Honesty** towards yourself and others,

- **Not misusing authority power**

- **Character** towards yourself and others.

I end this part of the chapter by mentioning that *your biggest obstacle is you, your mind and your control of yourself.* The more control you have, the less fighting toward breaking down the doubt in you, which also includes the fight against your laziness and your self-control. The more control you have, the stronger you will become, where your eye-contact and your hand-shake will be in alliance with your confidence.

ASPECTS TO ON DAILY

Taking care of yourself by training regularly is preferable. Movements make the blood flow and one positive effect will be that the brain performs better. This will in turn result in quality hours as well as having easier to concentrate. A notification: be aware that training may require walking or powerwalks as well, not just gym hours. The main focus is to feel healthy, the size is less important. The most important thing is that you love what you see in the mirror. And if you have children, you can play with them, which means that you do two things simultaneously: exercise and spending time with your loved ones. Additionally is a long-term diet preferable, where you decide a diet that you can live with, where you are allowed to eat candy or "junk-food" from time to time as a reward. It is like a normal working day. Do you really work for 8 hours straight or do you take coffee breaks too? – Clearly you take coffee breaks; it is the reward you get at work! These are two examples I know you can relate too, and my argument is the same either way: you must always reward yourself. If you are going to reach success – which I know you will – you need to give yourself awards for doing so great from time to time. Otherwise you will burn yourself out and as a result, not being able to cope with everything. My advice to you is to find a lifestyle that suits you, and you will see that your health, body and mind will feel good. The result will be a shining new you with a charisma stronger than before. Listen to your mind and your gut; it will lead you to accomplishment. So, my questions for you are: *How is your health? Do you exercise regularly and do you have a healthy diet?*

Moving on to a more important matter: what about your promises? Are you the one that always keeps her promises, or are you the kind of person that usually forgets or do not keep them at all? I am the first one: the one that always make sure to do everything in her power to keep her promises and the reason is because a promise means a lot to me. I grew up with parents that made me see the difference between a person that is reliable, and a person that is not. This included keeping my promises they said, as well as to always tell the truth. Even if it hurts the other part. Loyalty was one of the most important things that made us humans and separated us from animals they said. I am thinking back to when my parents' words fired back one time, where they could not keep one of their promises to my siblings and me. I recall us being sad that day, not knowing that they had important reasons for not being able to take us to Liseberg[13]. My father's mother had past away, and there we were, sad for not being able to go to an amusement park, when he lost his mother. A part from this time, they always kept their promises and we mirrored it. Loyalty became important for my better half and me, and is therefore one of the main six characteristics in the TSL-organization. Being a person that lie or cannot keep her promises will generate to people not believing what you say and therefore not count on your "empty promises". Just take the fable "The shepherd's son" written by Aesop as an example, where a shepherd boy lied a few times that the wolf was coming. The whole village tried to help him, but found in despair that he lied to them. The world works in wonders, am I right? Because in a soon future, the wolf indeed came, and when the wolf came and ate all the sheep, nobody believed him – and he therefore had nobody who could help him. This is the reason to why you need to be a woman of your word. Again, this is branding and by not keeping your promises, you will come off as a woman that is not trustworthy and not many people want to make business with that type of personality.

---

[13] *Liseberg: The largest amusement park in the Nordics.*

Behaviors such as holding doors for people and talking polite to elderly when you pass them by is always a behavior that will put a smile on a person's face. There is nothing wrong with making another human being smile. One behavior that will make you a lady of your word is to be on time – as I mentioned above. By being on time, you show the other part that you value her or his time and accept them giving it to you. However, occasions that are beyond your control can happen, which may result into you not being able to be on time. In occasions like these, enlighten the other part that you will be a minute late. This is done out of politeness, but also as a respect toward the other person. Additionally, if you have a family member, a colleague or a friend that is never on time, make sure to inform her or him that you value your time and that they should do the same. Keep the conversation by mentioning that you value his or hers by showing up on time and that they should do the same. This also shows the importance of you confronting a person if what he or she is doing is annoying you in any way. Also inform yourself that – at least according to my point of view – to constantly not being on time, you make yourself unreliable, and a lady shall avoid being labeled as unreliable in any circumstance. Therefore, always inform the other part if you are running late. Communication ladies, that is the key to success!

If someone embarrassed themselves in public, how do you react? My empathy is extremely big so I always make sure to help the person and not laugh at the occasion. I always make sure to not make a bigger deal than it is, simply because I always put myself in their shoes and how did I want people to react if I made a "fool" of myself? What I do is help the person in the best way possible, since I am a true believer of karma. What goes around will sooner or later come back around. Apart from this, a lady is also someone who speaks up when she believes in something, even if she is the only one believing it. We simply believe that she has confidence in her knowledge (and herself in general), which is the reason why she gives her statements, even though people can turn them down. But, she also knows that all humans have their own beliefs so she would never deny or force someone to believe or think in her ways. She is too confident in herself to do something like that. If somebody in the room does not like her ideas, she is confident staying with her statements. This goes hand in hand with people insulting you. How do you act or behave (in general) when someone is insulting you? Do you put up a front, or maybe you put up a show? I however make sure to give the person a chance to explain him- or herself, even though it may kill me inside. Or I at least try to be that person. This because I know that people make mistakes in the heat of the moment. And since I truly believe in karma, I also want someone to accept my chance to explain myself if I have done something to offend him or her. I also make sure to give him or her my view of the occasion, as well as how

158

they offended me. Always remember to be the bigger person. A part from this, I also make sure to point out that I will not accept that type of behavior again and this because a lady never let anyone stamp or insult her twice.

> *"To err is human; to forgive, divine!" – Alexander Pope.*

Moving on, aiming toward being polite, charming and gracious is something preferable. Reach toward being a person people love to discuss with, as much as laugh with. This means that you need to show your personality as well. You need to show your charisma and your other preferred behaviors, which is something I mentioned earlier. When thinking of it, people who tend to laugh and give away their personality by joking and having a great time are usually the ones that will go further in life. The reason why is because they make the conversation easier. These people know how to use their body as well as how to include the environment in the conversation. This simply means that these people have mastered the knowledge on how to communicate to make others interconnect after his or her wants. Something worth mentioning is to never, and I repeat never, look down on another person. Never think badly of a person just because he or she does not agree with you. The ones that think badly of others are just insecure in themselves. Remember that we are all equally born into this world and should be treated that way.

Lastly, private matters are meant to be private. Meaning: never do your laundry in public, even though it makes you frustrated. A lady has mastered her self-control fully, which also means that no one sees her "loosing it". Additionally does a true successful lady *never* rely on a man or another woman; she is a strong and independent woman. Do not get me wrong here. There is a difference in being dependent on and being interdependent with a person. The difference lays in the other part. Being dependent means that you are depending on his or her every move. Being interdependent means that you both are dependent on each other as well as being independent in your own skin. Interdependence is all about combining and thru that connection and work together, we will reach further than we would have alone. See the difference? You do not need to be independent to become a successful lady. You just need to find that man or woman you can be interdependent with. In a world dominating by men in all the big positions, remember that each man have an equal strong woman by his side, which makes her one of the biggest player. Just look at chess, the strongest chess piece is the queen where she does anything in her power to protect the king. This makes the king dependent on the queen's moves and on her knowledge, where a lady always make sure to increase her learning skills and knowledge to the fullest, as well as using them wisely. Keep that in mind the next time you have doubts about yourself and women in general.

HOW DID I BEHAVE TO GET THE RESPECT I DESIRED?

My behaviour made the job easier for me since I acted and behaved in a certain way, which led to the respect I desired. I had mastered my self and how to behave in the best way possible, as well as how to benefit from my advantages – that is the required behaviour you need to have. To become a person worthy of respect you need to work with your self and getting to know you, and this is done simply by working your way from the inside to the outside: inside out! By acknowledging and by controlling your self, your way of thinking and how you behave and see yourself, you will master the mental parts and then move on to the physical ones, where your charisma will enlighten your talk and act, which is the reason why I advice you to do the same. But you need to give it time and effort – remember that I have put all my effort into my self since I was a child, which took years to master. However, I also learned that, to be able to use this frequently, I needed to work with my self frequently. It is exactly like dieting. If you start on a diet and loose weight, you need to keep doing the same thing so you do not get it back. This said, if you start with your bad habits again, eventually will the weight come back on again. So what you need to do is to grow continuously and not forget to keep motivating yourself. Keep working with developing your self. Keep respecting yourself. Remember that I took a lot of downfalls regarding my self. It is never just a straight line. The road will be bumpy, but as long as you rise, that is all that matters in the end. You being able to stand up after a downfall say a lot about your character and your personality.

So, what are my advices for you? Firstly, never doubt yourself and your capabilities. By reading through this chapter, you should know about the self by now, where you should *never* doubt your knowledge or competences. Therefore, never settle down with a life you do not want just because you are "too afraid of making mistakes" or because you do not have the belief in yourself. Even if the people in our surrounding lack the belief in you, never doubt yourself. Always have in mind that *it is far better to go wrong in freedom than right in chains!*[14]. So my question for you is: "*Are you happy with yourself today?*" If the answer to that question is "no", you need to develop your inner self and go through this chapter, as well as the "*think*"-chapter once again. Step by step, with cautiousness so you can get the courage to change your thinking into making actions that will generate to you being happy with yourself and your life. Secondly, always listen to your heart – you are the one that needs to live with your decisions so make sure to make them in accordance to you dreams, not anyone else's. One thing you need to know is that people will try to influence your life everyday. It is your job to not let them control it. And never ask for permission regarding your life. It is yours and not theirs – make up your mind and

---

[14] *A quote written by Tomas Henry Huxley.*

pursue your wants and needs. Thirdly, always listen to your "gut" – your body knows what you want. Fourthly, never look at what everyone else is saying or doing – focus on you and put yourself first. Fifthly, always make sure to give your opinion on something (if you want to comment on something that is). A lady always makes sure to give her opinion – if she has one. This means that you shall eliminate those thoughts and aspects that pull you backwards, such as shyness. Do not get me wrong here. I said: if you had something to say. If not, then I would advice you to just stand there and participate in a non-verbal way. You do not need to have a verbal opinion on everything. Sixthly, make sure to help yourself before helping others – if you want to help people, you need to first make sure to help the person in the mirror. You need to be in one piece to be able to help another human being.

> *"I'm starting with the man in the mirror*
> *I'm asking him to change his ways*
> *And no message could have been any clearer*
> *If you want to make the world a better place*
> *Take a look at yourself, and then make a change"*
> *– Man in the mirror, by Michael Jackson*
> *(May him rest in peace).*

Lastly, be generous. You need to give back. If you give back, you will get more. A big example is my sister. She has always said that money is

163

just a number and that she is not attached to it because she does not want to be attached to material things. This is why she spent more money on me than on herself (which she still does by the way). She has mastered the true meaning with knowledge, time, power and money: that you should give back. Somehow, she always found ways to spend her advice and money on me and I always promised myself to give her everything because she deserves the world and beyond. We have always said "I love you to the moon and back" and that is exactly what we do with one another. I have learned that *"sharing is carrying"* since she shared everything with me and I shared everything with her. But, somewhere on the road, I lost myself and became a person I did not want to become. The stress, anxiety, loneliness and social phobia took a hold on me and I was lost in darkness – I got filled with negativity. She helped me through that darkness and made me see the light. She helped me thru that torture and I do as her nowadays – fill my mind with positive thoughts only. I give everything that I have: all my love and beyond to her. I will forever be grateful to her. She was the one that believed in me. So, today I share everything I have with her too, but no matter how much I spend on her, it will never be enough to what she has done for me. That is far more than I will ever be able to do for her. She filled my darkness with stars and then with only sunshine. It all started with stars in the sky, which is the reason I gave her two. So my conclusion here is: Sharing is carrying so make sure to share with people you care about – as long as they share their happiness with you.

164

Give and take ladies, do not only take.

Subsequently, after these advices and before diving into the next chapter, I have some question I need you to think trough carefully. The more honest you are, the easier will it be to let the past go and start the new life of your life tomorrow. A tomorrow already dealt with the past.

Question 1: *Who do you want to be?*

Do you want to be a lady that appreciates herself or a woman that does not have enough self-esteem, self-confidence and self-respect to actually believe in her self? On other terms: will you be the person that dares to dream big or will you be the one doubting that "that life" is for someone like you?

Question 2: *What shall we do to get there?*

When you know what you want to do and who you want to become, it is important to know how to get there. Usually is this done by giving everything you got into it – to commit yourself. Honestly speaking, to be someone you are proud of in this world, you need to put your whole heart and effort into what you are doing. With other words: you need to want it as much as you need breathing. You need to put not only everything you have, but also the heart and soul into it. Only then will you be able to reach and find greatness.

Question 3: *Why do you want that future for you? Why are you doing the thing you do to achieve those dreams by doing it that specific way you just choose?*

The reason I ask *why* is because you need to be able to answer why you want that future for you, and why you need to do what you need to do to get there. By acknowledging the why, you will be able to make it more real. If you cannot answer why, it will be more like an illusion you have, rather than a vision. By being truthful to your self by answering the why, you will make it more real and therefore change your mindset into working even harder towards achieving it.

After answering these questions honestly, you need to always remember that a person always has choices. You are just narrowing your view. If you just open your eyes, you will be able to see the peripheral view, which will lead to a bigger picture and you will ultimately realize that one answer is never the only right answer. People have a lot of options. As Harvey Specter in the TV-show "Suits" said: *"You do what they say or they shoot you, right? Wrong! You take the gun. You pull out a bigger gun or you call their bluff or you do one of another 146 other things"*. However, I want you to bear in mind that imagination is something worth firing up too, since it usually brings people success. Just look at what imagination did to JK Rowlings, the author of the Harry Potter series. Fantasy and imagination pays off. But more importantly, she believed in herself and her books, and never gave up on her dreams until she got what she wanted. That is a true successful lady spirit! I do see a correlation between big dreams and even bigger actions, which is the right mindset of a lady. Remember that big names such as Steve Jobs, Bill Gates, Serena Williams and Oprah Winfrey all had big dreams, followed by even bigger actions. Those actions are why they achieved what they wished for: they dared to act in A-style!

As you see, our behaviour defines ourselves. Furthermore, it is safe to say that the people that have bigger self-awareness achieve more since they know what they want. Additionally is it worth mentioning that it is all in your head, which means: the way you think regarding yourself and the environment in general. The previous chapter was the biggest one, for the very reason that it all starts and ends with how you think regarding the special act and matter. The communication between you and your brain, which is proof toward the "thinking" part being one of two most important ones, followed by behaviour, which is the second biggest one simply because it contains so much learned and taught behaviours (both mentally and physically). Our actions and behaviour are influenced by our childhood and therefore: how we grew up, where we grew up, and what type of thinking we have regarding different aspects. Did you have someone who constantly pushed you into the darkness or you maybe lived in a small town with a lot of gossiping? It is all affected by your youth which means that your actions and behaviours can be explained by your yesterdays, where what type of childhood you had growing up have its impact on you, where the society, culture, religion, friends, neighbours and family all have a part in your character and personality today.

By now I think you are aware of what I want to highlight with these two chapters, am I right? Yes, you got it right, successful lady. I want you to get to know *you*, and you are on your way. You are on your way becoming the one you have always dreamt of, secretly or openly. Either way, you are on your way. And as we have finished reading these two chapters, we have come a long way in our growth toward your self-development and showing the world who you are. You are doing great successful lady. Keep on reading. We want to make you the next star.

Behaviors behaviors, behaviors. Whether we were born in this country or that, whether we were born as a girl or a boy, whether we were born in this socioeconomic class or that, whether we were born in the city or on the country-side, whether we were born a right- or a left hander, whether we were born with this parents or that, whether we were born with a desire to love a girl or a boy, whether we were born light-headed or dark-headed, whether we were born with this genes or that, and whether we were born a dualist or not. It all says something about our current state. Did we have a hard time growing up or not? Did our parents love us? Did our friends trait us? Did we trait ourselves? Did our environment think of us as an equal or not? Did the environment influence us into hating our hair and eyes due to our differences? Did people highlight your similarities or your differences? Did you grow up liking your reflection, or did you end up getting influenced – creating an inside that matched those outside accusations? Did you in the end, come to loose yourself? And did you live in a dilutive world simply because a living in delusion is far easier to deal with than a life in destruct? Was your reality that hard that you in the end came to stop looking ahead?

Everything that happened to us in our childhood influenced our behaviors, which will influence our actions. Every occurrence, every event, and every occasion today will influence how we look at things

169

tomorrow. Therefore, make sure to deal with the traumas that reflect wrongly. Therefore, make sure to deal with your past to be able to change your behaviors, which will – as a result – change our actions towards the better.

ACT

"The only way out is through" – Robert Fast

Our actions are influenced by both our thoughts and behaviours. Our thoughts and behaviours influences the way we interpret with things, all affected by how we have been taught to think and behave. Simply put: behaviour from our experiences and youth leads to actions influenced by these taught thoughts and behaviours.

As we have mentioned in the "behaviour"- chapter: if behaviour is more about *"in general"*, the act is more about the moment. Think: "behave yourselves in particular" and "act accordingly due to a specific occasion". What I mean by this is that behaviours are something we got taught from our environment and is therefore something that influences our current actions. A "great impression" is something we all have had to deal with, whether it was to behave in the family dinner, meet your partner's parents or maybe just impress our employer. However, I want you to have some things in mind whenever you want to make a great imprint on others. Knowing how to put on a smile is something everyone probably got taught by their parents. However, this smile can be used differently in certain circumstances. Positive attitude is also

171

something we got taught from our parents. Or at least my parents taught me a lot of manners, which I believe yours did too. These are learned behaviours that we imprint from the people in our surroundings during growing up. But, when it comes to actions, both these two things mentioned above (smile and positive attitude) need to be adapted to the situation. As a lady, you need to master the ability on *how* to act in different circumstances: acknowledging what the situation requires from you, and your actions might need to be complete different in two different situations. You simply need to read the situation and see what type of occasion this is, as well as knowing what type of people you are dealing with. By knowing this, you will make an impression based on the situation, rather than making the situation being based on you. Since we want to make a great impression, our act needs to be based on how the other part sees us. By analysing the circumstances and behave accordingly – by taking full use of both your behavioural knowledge as well as thinking knowledge – is how you act in line with a successful lady (think of the looking glass self). So, you need to have basic knowledge into observing a situation and what that occasion expects from you. And try to remember:

"A lady knows just what to do in any circumstance".

REFLECTING THE BEST VERSION AND SIDE OF YOUSELF

Even though it takes more energy from time to time, a lady always ends up with knowing how to act in any circumstance. The reason why is because she listens actively. Because of her active listening, she will be able to follow the conversation. She does not only do this for herself though, she does it more for the opponent. Honestly speaking, when you make gestures that you are following what the opponent is saying, you will be able to signal that you are there with them – in that time and space. This will make the other person feel valued, since you are giving them all your attention. Apart form this, smiling needs to be highlighted in these occasions as well. You need to understand that your smile affects your health in a positive way, which also means that you affect the opponent in the same way. Thanks to mirror neuron, we influence the other person by smiling. This genuine smile will trigger their mirror neuron and that will lead to them not only smiling back, but feel the smile and the emotions the smile brings with. In my point of view, this is a win-win situation. Conversely, there is also other aspects that needs to be taken into consideration. Some occasions requires you to act like you were not bothered by what the person said or did (in that specific situation). Even though you might not like the situation you have put yourself in, keep it to yourself. I have been around people that always complaint and we do not want to be associated with people who complain, do we? We would rather be associated with proactiveness than reactiveness – or we should rather prefer to be associated with those characteristics – which is why a lady should acts toward controlling whatever she can change, instead of reacting in forms of complaints. Therefore, make sure to take the matters in your own hands. If the problem is too small to even give it you attention, then it is not worth you time, nor your energy for that matter. Remember that people tend to judge you, and by hearing your complaints, you will bring down their mood too. And let us be honest here, they really do not care about it either, and will as a result begin to avoid you instead. This will by the way also destroy your branding. Think *Word-of-mouth* (WOM) ladies. WOM is extremely powerful, where 9 positive WOM equals 1 negative WOM. So make sure to not give them any bad things to talk about behind your back.

BE OPEN (CONFIDENT) ABOUT WHAT YOU WANT

If you want to start a conversation with a person you never spoken to before, make sure that he or she knows it. This can be done with the non-verbal communication, which we will be talking more about in the "talk"-chapter. But for now, while focusing on smiling at her or him at the same time as you maintain a strong eye contact, half the battle is done. You can then sense if the other part wants to speak to you. If you see any openness in the opponent's body language, you approach that person. There is nothing such as a confident girl – confidence is actually the most valuable accessory a woman can wear. That combined with a smile, at least according to the TSL-organization.

If you, on the other hand, happen to make a bad impression on someone by being on a bad mood, you can always change it to something good by using your humour and say something like "I'm sorry. We had a bad start, which could be explained by my bad mood. I see you meet me before dinner". Hopefully she or he accepts the apology. If they do not like your apology, use your knowledge from the previous chapters to change their minds about you. Additionally, let the coming chapters have a say in that too. Sometimes the situation requires you to be more head-forward and actually give an apology. Let us say, if you have made a bad first impression – all based on something you said or did – make sure that you apologise for your actions. We all have been there and we all know the hangover feeling or the feeling of misjudging a person or a situation in some kind of way (not knowing the story behind their actions). What you could do to save the situation is apologising. This could be done by saying something like "My sincerest apologies for my behaviour a second ago. You see, I do not do well with hunger. Not that I should let it go out on you, but let me buy you a "fika"[15] and get to know one another. Let's make a fresh start". This straightforward apology would send the signals that you are mature, but also that you

---

[15] *Fika is the Swedish word for coffee breaks.*

want to put an effort into getting to know the other person. Additionally, that you take responsibility for your actions. Also bear in mind that this is give and take. If someone made a bad impression on you, accept their apology when they want to make amends. Always try to put yourself on the other person's shoes. Remember, for some people it is not easy to give an apology. Try to make it easier for them by showing that you are listening to their apology and meet them half way. Again, try to be the bigger person. Always remember that every person is worth a second chance. We all make mistakes. After all, we are all humans. But it is when these second changes become to many and therefore turns to a habit that we have a problem. One time is no time. But three or four times? That should be considered a habit.

TREAT OTHERS AS YOU WISH TO BE TREATED

The golden rule "treat others as you would like to be treated" is a great rule to live by. Karma advice you to live in similar patterns: you will be treated the way you treat people. However, obstacles will continuously come in your way, and what you need to do is to see them as tests, not as a curse or problems. By solely switching mindset, you will have a whole different view on everything that comes in your way. Again, this is the power of positive thinking. Also, always stand by your beliefs, even if the whole crowd think otherwise. Since debates are discussions on a particular matter in public meetings, I think there should be no right or wrong in debates. This means, stick to what you value and give

176

your arguments to why you think the way that you do, as well as why you value those decisions. If you think B is right, you shall stand up for that answer, instead of accepting A. And by the way, by not giving an argument against A, you are quietly accepting A as your answer. It may also turn out that B was the better answer and there you were, having the knowledge but was too shy or insecure to even make that statement. However, I can relate to this type of acting since I have been there, constantly insecure in my capabilities and myself. Not to forget not having the guts to stand against the flow, even though I knew I was right. Confidence is something you will get the more you know about you and your abilities, which is why I today speak up my mind whenever I do not seem to agree. I do not make a scene, I simply just speak my mind. It does not have to be uglier than that. So try to speak up your mind – you are a confident lady. You can do it. I am betting on you!

Furthermore, what do you ladies out there think of people talking about you in your absence? You do not like it, am I right? That is what I figured. Neither do I. And this is something really important to bear in mind. Never – and I repeat never – talk about a person who is not present. This sends out bad signals to the rest of the people in your surroundings. And let us be honest. If these people talk about people who are not there with you, do you not think that they will be talking

177

behind your back as soon as you leave? As I figured! Just to put it out there, people who is making a living by talking about others when they are not around are not my kind of people. Neither should they be yours. Try to remember that people who are friends depending on their similar dislikes, will always stay like that – a disliked "friendship". Or as I call them: dislikeship. And these dislikeships are a group of negative thinkers who focus on whom did what instead of focusing on their lives and their own developments. These people are not people you should be associated with, my future successful lady. You should not make it harder for yourself to think positive and handle your own business. As soon as you have seen where the problem relies, remove that temptation. It is like a habit. If you are used to sit on the phone until late in the night, then it is a habit. What you in that case should do is to remove that temptation and you will see that those long nights by the phone instead will be long hours of good night sleep.

WHAT TO DO WITH OUR SO CALLED "OBSESSION" WITH OUR PHONES?

In today's society, we are constantly texting, talking on the phone, surfing and being social on social media. Even when other people accompany us, we seem to find our phone and our absent friends more important than the one next to us. Are we forgetting to live by in the moment? This is why it is more important than ever to act like a lady when you are using your phone in peoples' closeness. My opinion, you should not use the phone when other people accompany you. The reason for this is because you need to show your company more interest than your phone. So what I am trying to tell you is to give your complete attention to the people that are accompanying you, where your phone should be on silent and in your purse. If you are waiting for an important call, make sure that the person you are out with knows that you are waiting for someone to reach you, so you can be excused when this call arrives. *So, how do I do when I am out with company?* -Well, first off, I make sure to have my phone on silent mode and in my purse or wallet. I do use my phone from time to time, but this is when my company is away on a phone-call or maybe in the ladies room. Most of the time I just give my phone a glance and then it goes back in to the purse, and that is how it should be. This signals that you are present with your company. If you are constantly using your phone, why did you not stay in?

THE CRAZY DRIVING LADY

I believe, you as much as me, have been experiencing the situation when you have been stuck in traffic with a yelling person. Well, traffic do have a beauty in bringing out the best in people, do you not agree? In this frustrated situation, every one in the traffic is indeed being idiots. Are they not? Everyone. Except you, right? Well, let us change the scenario. What if you happen to be the yelling and frustrated person that is driving the car? You still think that everyone in the traffic is being irresponsible and not taking into consideration that you are in a hurry? Now, in these circumstances they are more idiots, are they not? You start yelling and calling the car next to you names, as if that will make you feel better and be on time. These so called "beautiful" actions we take on in traffic is not giving us anything, so what we basically do is that we are being reactive instead of being proactive. In these circumstances, when you are stuck in the traffic, is it hard to be proactive since you cannot do anything about it and you are too caught up with being irritated by the traffic, which means your own feelings and no one else. But you need to be aware of the fact that you are stuck in this not so wonderful situation together. What could you do really? Go out of the car, lift it over your head and walk past the entire traffic until you reach the red light? Unfortunately, this is not even an opportunity since we are not living in a world where supernatural people such as the hulk exists. This example makes me think of the 80's when people walked with a radio on their shoulders and listened to the music. This thought always makes me laugh. People actually did that. But, since we have agreed on that traffic making us be reactive instead of proactive, I have two things I use to do whenever I am stuck in the traffic. Fist, I always have a book in by bag. You never know when you have the time to read it. For me, a stuck traffic is just a perfect situation. Even if the car behind me tends to use their car whistles more than usual. Second, I listen to podcasts. Why not take the opportunity to

180

actually learn something while you have the time. Besides, now you just listen to someone talking, which actually not really requires you writing or working. But still, you are learning and will as a result perhaps learn something you would not have if you would not have been stuck in that traffic. I actually have a third thing I use to do, but this requires me avoid being in that situation. This is, taking the metro or walking. Not only is the metro making me avoid the hectic traffic, it also takes me from A to B faster than a car can possible do. Additionally, its more global friendly.

I want to end this chapter by mentioning:

"Your behaviours and actions highlight the importance in the affection you have on the people in your surrounding, but also a reflection on your self-confidence and how you feel about yourself in general. You are your actions, you are your habits, and you are how you treat other people. In short: you are what people see and those actions reflect the real you. Therefore, make sure to act *like a successful lady."*

PART 3

TALK THE WALK & WALK THE TALK.

Imagine yourself saying the right things in the right occasions. Imagine people looking at you with those eyes. You know which eyes I am talking about, do you not? Yes, you are right. Those eyes that you use when you look at someone you admire. Yes, you are getting this straight. Now you are realizing that people admire you too. But, *why do they admire me* you keep asking yourself, and in which circumstances? Well, honestly, they admire you because you know how to get your message across. You know you, so you ultimately look for those similarities in people and act on that. Yes, you are self-aware and aware of other people too. And therefore you have mastered the way to communicate after this awareness too. People look at your communication with clarity and you then realize that it is not only what you say, is it? It is also *how* you say it. So basically they admire not only your spoken words, but also how good you are at getting your message across, with the help of your non-verbal communication.

Yes, you have mastered how to think like a lady, how to behave like a lady and how to act like a lady. Now it is time to master how to talk like a lady since this image I just painted up in your mind is just all that: communication in A-style!

TALK

"Communication means sharing together, thinking together, not agreeing or disagreeing together but thinking, observing, learning, understanding together. Both you and the speaker have to take the journey together" – J. Krishnamurti.

Communication includes both non-verbal communication and verbal communication. This chapter will merely focus on the non-verbal communication, where it will include both branding and the ability to speak in front of people. As you can tell by the sentences above, interactions are not solely done with words (verbal), but most of the things we *say* are actually spoken by our bodies. With this said, the verbal communication is associated with our expressions with words. The non-verbal, on the other hand, is correlated with expressions and gestures made by our body movements and facial expressions. In addition are both touching and clothing a type of non-verbal communication. Even the sound from your spoken words is seen as a non-verbal communication, which further shows the connection between the verbal and non-verbal signals. This said, people usually judge you by the non-verbal communication you radiate, which make the non-verbal part more important than the verbal. But apart from the description above is the non-verbal communication also the interaction between itself and both dressing, posture and walking. As you see,

185

everything links together in a good way. We just need all these parts to be in alliance. As a story needs to follow a red thread, does our non-verbal communication also need to tell a story on its own – simultaneously.

When it comes to communication, try to always have an open dialog with the opponents. Think about it, is it not preferable to have someone listening to you with an open communication, where his or her body language welcomes what you say – instead of having someone in front of you having a closed body language, which can radiate that they do not agree with what you say, or that they simply are not there with you mentally? When speaking about closed communication, this actually is your body's way of communicating with the surrounding of what you are thinking – subconsciously – which shows that a person that sits with his arms crossed usually is shut of when it comes to the subject, or he just disagrees with what has been said. However, if you want to have a smoother communication, try to unfold those arms, as well as those legs. This will give the opponent the expression that you are fully there and listen to what he or she has to say. This will also, as a result, make the communication more smooth and easy to both the giver and the taker. Just think of it yourself next time you are in a conversation: how will you feel when the person in front of you is closed off (distanced) from the conversation? You will be a bit frustrated, will you not? Therefore, make sure to use that you yourself have an open

186

communication with your opponent to make the communication you between more smooth. And since we are talking about the non-verbal, it is a great time to dive into the world of non-verbal communication.

"The way we talk, walk, sit and stand all say something about us, and whatever is happening on the inside can be reflected on the outside"
— Karen Watchman

However, before diving into the chapter's first focus, I want you to think something thru. I want you to be self-aware. Therefore, I want you to ask yourself: *How do you speak and what do you include in your speaking? Do you put any emphasis on either the tone or the grammar? Or maybe you highlight your knowledge when you speak? Do you include your whole body in the conversation too, or do you keep it simple? You maybe talk a lot with your hands instead? Or maybe you are not aware of it yet?* Write it down and when you are finished, let us keep on reading: We are going to make you a star!

NON-VERBAL COMMUNICATION

"Non-verbal communication is an elaborate secret code that is written nowhere, known by none, and understood by all." — Edward Sapir.

The non-verbal communication is the communication you radiate without words. This is therefore the communication that you signal when you walk by, or just stand there – dominated by both your dressing and walking, as well as your attitude toward these aspects, which is shown in your posture. I would say, in one sentence, that the non-verbal communication means *how to express yourself without using verbal sentences but communication in any other sort: gestures and facial expressions, mimics as well as the vocal chords.* The non-verbal communication is used to express our feelings, where it is used as a complement, as well as emphasize or clarification to the verbal communication.

Did you know that – according to Albert Mehrabian – 55 precent of the communication is seen in a person's body language, their voice stands for 38 precent of the communication, and their spoken words stands for only 7 precent of the communication? – By using your body language to your advantage, you can make a big impact on the people in your surrounding. According to Mark Cowden, a person does get judged in the first four seconds. All people do this subconsciously and by focusing on your body language, you can make sure that they judge you in a way that you want to be judged. Mark Cowden further mentions that we put people into four categories; friends, foe, potential partner or indifferent: the ones that do not match either of the three mentioned above. So, by focusing on the way you walk into a room as well as your postures, you can control whether the rest of the encounter goes well or poorly for you.

188

We have all heard the countenance "express yourself", right? I certainly have, but mostly in areas such as art or poetry. However, you need to understand that we are expressing ourselves all the time, which can be comparable to art. In the non-verbal case, you are the pencil drawing your own painting. In your case is this particular art drawn by your clothing and other communication tools such as your body language, walking and vocal chords. With other words: how you interact with the society in the chosen non-verbal interactions. We all have those friends who are able to be friends with anyone, right? Or maybe you are one of those people? As we mentioned in earlier chapters do these people have a charisma. But what I did not mention before is that this charisma influences the surrounding in a positive way, since these people tend to radiate optimism. The surrounding gets the positive vibes and considers this person to be a great one, where they will talk about her in a positive way, even mention words like: "Well, I got a great expression of her. Gotta love that energy tho'". This thing they mentions as "energy" is basically this person's body language, vocal chords, but also her behaviour in general. In short: it is what she radiates. If this example does not make you aware of the importance in your communication, I do not know what will.

Still not satisfied? Then I will give you clearance. We have all been in familiarity with those women who steal the attention wherever they go, are we not? We are acquaintances with them in one way or another. These people are women like us, where they are someone's mother, someone's sister, someone's wife or someone's world. Everywhere they go, people tend to look at them with a sparkle in their eyes. They have ultimately judged these people by their walk, their dressing and their communication in general. This in turn sends signals that these people absorb and judge from "these people's cover", which is usually to their advantages since their personality and clothing represents their 'successful lady'-character. This without them even opening their mouth, which also means that these people never spoke to them verbally. The people in the surrounding just assumed by their non-verbal communication. They assumed but what they might not have had a clue on is that this person probably wanted them to think and judge her in the way that the surrounding did. By using her knowledge on how to talk, act, behave and think, she gets the environment to give her the reaction she wants from them. Solely this acknowledges makes this communication skill one of the most important ones for a successful lady since we need to signal the right signs. This is also why your communication with yourself is *the* most important one. The respect these ladies in turn gets from the judgements gives them status and access to a higher life – etiquette and a higher confidence too, which gives them – in turn – courage to go after everything they wish for. But

190

be aware. As I mentioned briefly just one sentence above, these ladies know that these types of results do not come without the most important communication. They know that this would not be possible without their communication to *themselves*. These successful ladies simply know that they need to be in alliance with themselves to be able to radiate what they want to highlight with their own self, which will in turn be what the world sees. Shortly put: what is happening on the inside will be shown on the outside and by having an alliance within, you will be having an alliance inside out too.

"Fie, fie upon her! There's language in her eyes, her cheek, her lip. Nay, her foot speaks; her wantom spirits look out at every joint and motive of her body"
– William Shakespeare.

We mentioned in the introduction part of this chapter an open communication and a closed one. But what do these two things really mean? What is considered an open body language and what is considered a closed one? Since we do not want to have a closed body language, I think we should start with this one, only to end with what we want to put emphasis on. So, starting off with closed communication. This basically means that you shut yourself off from the conversation subconsciously. This can be done by – and this is the most common one – either folding your arms or legs. I know that some of you will give a comment that goes something like: "Well, that is basically the most comfortable way of sitting/standing. What should I do with the hands/legs if I do not fold them?" – Well, honestly speaking, it is more preferable (and more respectful towards the opponent) to have your hands on your lap, with your legs unfolded. This because it gives away a more give and take communication, where you are open to what the opponent says. When it comes to the comfortable part, you are subconsciously doing this because you have been wired to act that way in these sorts of gatherings. This said, you have programmed yourself into acting this way. Therefore, knowing what happened to a person during their childhood can help people understand why they act or communicate in the ways that they do. So, correlating this to your folding, you have been programing your mind to fold your arms whenever you are in a situation you do not feel comfortable in. Maybe you have been shut off too many times before, or shut down? Maybe you do not think that your mind matters and therefore protect yourself from harm? Or maybe it is something else? Since this is something you taught yourself, it is also something you can un-teach yourself and replace it with something else. Undo and redo! The TSL-organizations suggestion would be to always have your hands on your lap, where you can hold one over the other. When you stand, the arms could be resting on the sideways. This is also good when it comes to taking up more space, since that will radiate confidence. But to radiate

192

confidence, you need to have your weight on both legs. This since nobody can rub you off your guard that easily (both mentally and physically). But – and this in an important but – if you have a skirt, you cannot really do anything about it. Put one of your legs over the other when sitting (to protect your valuable part) and make sure that your folding the one furthest away from the opponent. This is signalling that you shut of the environment and focuses on her or him.

Thus, apart from folding your arms and legs, closed communication can also be associated with a body turned away from the opponent, as well as lack of eye-contact and fidgeting. Fidgeting is your body's way of dealing with anxiety, which shows the surrounding that there is something bothering you. It could be something about the conversation or something the conversation made you think of. Either way, it shows lack of presence. What you should do is deal with your anxiousness; why this topic, this occurrence, or this person might bring anxiety to your table. But since these are subconscious behaviour and in most cases are hidden from us, you first need to be aware of the fidgeting in order to be aware of what causes your fidgeting. Therefore, be ware of it first and then try to eliminate it by knowing why you have those habits and deal with those reasons. A habit is exactly that – a habit. And since habits are patterns, they are hard to break. Therefore give it time. Additionally is eye contact preferable, where you can nod to show that you are following what is being said. Golden stars will come to the ones that even engage to a point where they ask follow-up questions.

These are some of many closed communication signals. If I had brought all of them up here, this chapter would have been really long. And since we want to put focus on other aspects as well, I chose these ones because these are the ones we observe the most. So, to sum it up, if you have your body shut off, you might come off as someone that does not agree to what is being said – someone that is not there mentally, and someone that dislike this situation in some or many ways. And the opponent might be offended by it, simply because she or he might have been up all night preparing for this meeting, and there you are, all caught up in your own state of mind, dilemma or dissatisfaction. This is not fair to neither of you. Therefore, if you are not going to be there 100%, make sure to reschedule or something similar. Otherwise you will come off as a "not so present or friendly" person, and your branding will be cluttered by that act. Therefore, try to meet the opponent half way and always think of how you would want the opponent to communicate in your presence. Be open minded, and you will se that your body will be open too.

SOME NON-VERBAL COMMUNICAITON TO KEEP IN MIND:
Now when we have talked briefly about non-verbal communication, I think its time to focus on some of the non-verbal signals worth keeping

in mind. The signals we will highlight are: body movements, postures, gestures, facial expressions, vocal chords, eye-contact and clothing: starting off with body movements and work down to the clothing.

Body movements show the way you walk: the purposiveness in your walking, as well as the speed. If you see a lady passing by with a high speed and swinging arms, you can sense purposiveness. If you, on the other hand, see a lady passing by all churched and silent, you can sense shyness and insecurity in her walking. This shows that our movements need to be with confidence. The reason you need confidence in your walking is because you can spot a persons personality a mile away, where the people that walk with confidence seems to be the ones with higher self-esteem and self-efficacy, as well as higher self-confidence. So, by only looking at a person's walk or the way she sit, you can spot her confidence a mile away, as well as where she is headed: both literally and in terms of goals. And honestly speaking, the way you sit and stand – your posture – will also give away your feelings and state. Something worth mentioning is that the way you sit and stand can change your emotional state too. This is something my role model Tony Robbins supported as well, where he mentioned that emotions are created by motions. This leads to us mentioning that slouching is one of the gestures that will bring you down emotionally, and the "superman stand" will enlighten you emotionally. So make sure to have a good posture so you can influence your emotions, as well as giving a great impression to the people in your surrounding. Therefore, make sure to have a positive walk, since that walk will influence your emotions in a positive way.

However, an important note is that your walking is influenced by your view on yourself too. If you are insecure, if you are shy or if you have confidence in yourself, this can easily be shown. This is proof toward your walking being persuaded by your personality and your inside too, which shows that you need to make sure to treat yourself good and not give yourself the benefit of a doubt. Believe in yourself and your capabilities, and your walking will be a reflection of that. And you know what happens then? Yes, then people will believe in you too!

"Your walk is the reflection of you, so make sure to have a behaviour that matches a true successful lady, and as a result, so will your walking be."

A notification: it is important to walk with confidence and attitude, yes, but still keep your feet on the ground. Your self-confidence and self-esteem needs to be shown in your steps so you can get the right charisma. However, it is important to see the difference between believing in yourself by having a good self-esteem and self-confidence, and thinking that you are better and more beautiful than everyone else.

196

It is a difference between having self-esteem and self-confidence, and being an egoist and narcissist. Know the difference and if you happen to be the second mentioned one, this is something you need to eliminate asap[16]! You are not better than the others; we are all humans and shall be treated equally.

Postures are a type of body language which we can analyze from, completely focused on how you sit and stand. For example, if you are in a conference room, the lady that is leaned forward is usually the one engaged in the subject, as well as really interested in what the boss or her colleagues has to say. In this conference room, you will also see people widen their territory, which is a sign of confidence. Your expanding radiates your confidence in both yourself, and the environment – as well as in the topic that is being held. So, the more these people widen their body language, the higher their confidence is. You will also be able to analyze which ones that are more bored in the moment and which ones that lack focus; you just have to read what their bodies express. This is how the reader can be able to identify those who lack interest in what she has to say, as well as those who put focus into what she has to say. The people who lack interest are usually turned away, bodily or metaphorically. If you are turned metaphorically, it means that you are probably somewhere else with your mind, which can

---

[16] *Asap = as soon as possible*

be seen in your face and body. This is something we mentioned before, when we spoke about open communication and closed communication. The lady that is closed off is usually dominated by closed communication. Either by looking in another direction, having the body turned on another direction, and/or shut of by folding arms and legs. Apart from this can your folding also radiate shyness or insecurity. Since we usually make ourselves smaller when we are insecure, a person's folding and "taking up less space" could be taken as proof toward them feeling insecure in the topic, occurrence or in themselves.

Gestures are more about how we use our hands, arms and body in whole when we talk. If you are a person that keeps her hands behind your back, usually this signals to the outsiders that you are the one in charge. But be ware: when you hold your hands behind your back, you immediately become a target of doubt in the opponent eyes since we usually are afraid or interested in why that person does not show her or his hands. "What are they hiding?" is usually a question that pup up in our mind subconsciously when we do not see hands. Since cave time have the human species been expressing our fear by first looking at the opponents' hands, to see if they are a friend or a foe. This is the reason why I advice you to keep your hands in the opponents sight, so you do not let them end up focusing on other aspects than on what you want them to put their focus on. Furthermore, keep yourself away from worrying, which will reduce your fidgeting as well. This is also were

198

your unfolding comes to play. Your open gestures will show the opponent that you are fully there. If you are in a conversation where the other part is talking, and your nodding from time to time, you show this person that you are following and agreeing on what he or she has to say. And now you might ask me: *So, what's the difference between posture and gesture?* – The answer I would give you is that gestures is usually one movement or part of the body you focus on, while posture is more about how you stand or sit, which mean the body all together.

Facial expressions are important. You can show a lot of gestures in your face. Additionally, putting them all together and you will be reading a person's mood easily. You can see a happy face from a far, as well as an angry or a sad one. The muscles in the face are changing all the time, dependent solely on your current state of emotion. Eyebrows, mouth, cheek, forehead and eyes are the parts that are in interaction with one another – to be able to express the feelings correctly. The facial expressions are usually the hardest yet the easiest ones to control, since that is the source of most information as well as the point where we put our focus on when it comes to controlling our reactions to what is being said – emotionally speaking. But that is not the biggest reason. The biggest reason is because the face shows so much information – directly. These emotions at once will make it harder to control too, be ware of it. When we feel, we show. But, as a lady, you need to be able to try to reduce some of the negative emotions from the opponent's eyes by eliminating it from yours if those occurrences happen. We all have been in situations that bring up the worst in us. In situations like these, I want you to be self-aware and take control of yourself: have self-control. This is something you will manage when you know your behaviors. Remember that people tend to remember you for your expressions. If you are a lady who is constantly angry, that is what people will remember you for since they think this is your personality trait. So, make sure to have a more positive emotional expression on the face and people will start to see you as a more friendly face. And therefore, as a person they would like to be around more often. And always remember that emotions are cautious. If you feel happy, people in your surroundings will feel happy too – and therefore, love your presence since you bring happiness with you.

Moving on to *the voice*. It is important to mention that the voice includes everything beyond the spoken words. With the help of the tone, you will be able to sense if a person is excited, happy, angry or depressed in that moment when those words were spoken. However, this cannot be done without the intonation, pitch or the volume behind the words. This is why a clear language is more preferable, as well as the pauses we make while speaking. The reason why the voice is considered a non-verbal signal is because it is a way for us to read what is beyond the meaning of the spoken words, so-called paralanguage[17]. By having a presentation filled with ups and downs in your volume, by having pitches and by giving more intonation on the more important word in specific areas, the language will be clearer and it will be easier to follow thru as a listener. As a lady you need to be willing to express your feelings with pauses as well. It is important to know when it is time for a pause and give the opponent time to think of what just have been said. After that pause you can continue with the presentation. To master this, you need to keep practice, practice, practice, and practice – like you need to do with everything else. Think in terms of dialog instead of monolog and think of doing it naturally instead of forcing it.

"When the eyes say one thing, and the tongue another,
a practiced man relies on the language of the first" – Paul J. Meyer

Eye contact is a topic I have been taught since I was a child. When my parents talked to me, they wanted me to look them straight in the eyes. The reason why they wanted me to keep an eye contact with them was not to intimidate me, but to make sure that I was fully there, in the same conversation as they were. This way, they could see if I was following

---

[17] *Paralanguage is included in the non-verbal communication since it helps a person realize what is being said, without focusing on the words that are being spoken. Paralanguage therefore refers to the tone of a person's voice.*

what was being said or if I was there mentally, and if I was not, when they lost me. They simply wanted me to understand what they told me. Since I was daydreaming most of the time, my parents made sure that when they talked, my siblings and I needed to nod and make gestures that radiated that we followed what was being said – which included the contact eye-wise. They also taught my siblings and me from a young age that confidence is shown thru a person's eye contact, and the insecurity in lack thereof. This said, they tried to teach me from an early age to be confident in what was being said – or what was being heard. I never understood what eye contact had to do with confidence until I came across books that explained how your behavior influences your communication. Despite having that knowledge, I still had a hard time keeping eye contact. Since I was shy as a kid, I had a tough time not tearing myself into pieces when I looked my teachers or older people in their eyes. The reason why was because I was too afraid of getting judged and that frightens increased the anxiety within. I did not want them to burn me again. And since I did not want to get burned, my insecurity made me look away the second I laid eyes on the opponent. But, since I needed to do it out of respect and since eye contact helps the interactions quality two people between, I knew I needed to try to look my teacher into her or his eyes. I further came to grow with the knowledge that a strong eye contact made me seem more qualified and more knowledgeable in the topic that was being spoken about, trustworthier, and lastly, more emotionally stable. The last was where I

202

lacked the most since I was not stable at all. I never dealt – fully dealt – with my inside, and therefore did not have any stable emotions. So that is what I focused on. I dealt with my inside and in the end I got confidence enough (in myself and the subject). I dealt with my inferiority complex. This breakthrough led to increased eye contact by having more confidence in both myself and the topic, the communication became more qualitative too, and lastly, the interaction became more pleasant and positive. This shows that a shy kid has a harder time keeping eye contact, as well as an insecure one. But if I could break that pattern, so can you. If I can break free, so can you! If you are one of those people that are either shy or insecure, you need to do as I did. Deal with your past and your confidence will be shown in your communication. I am aware of the fact that most of you have been punished for different reasons and I know that those actions might have broken you down. That makes you vulnerable and uncomfortable. That makes you want to hide and be invisible. I know because I used to be there. I used to not look people in their eyes because I was too insecure in myself and was always afraid that they might punish or judge me if I did. If I did not look into people's eyes, I hoped they would leave me alone. But I practiced. I dealt with it – and I mastered myself. I changed perception. If you teach yourself to keep eye contact without flaring with the eyes, you will signal confidence and success. On the other hand, if you do flare, you will give the other the knowledge of your uncertainty in you. Also in the opponents, the environment or the situation, which is what we want to reduce – why you feel that uncertainty in the first place. But you have to bear in mind that in some cultures it is considered impolite to look older people straight in their eyes. So whenever you visit some other countries with different cultures, make sure to do your homework. As I mentioned before: When in Rome, do as the Romans do.

Lastly, your *clothing* is also a non-verbal communication. What you wear says a lot about you, whether it is a jacket, shoes, a hat or a bag: it all says a lot about your character. Our clothing radiates to the extent as gestures, postures, facial expressions and walking does. Everything you radiate is a signal – signals that will be interpreted by the environment. However, I want to highlight that we need to be careful when we read peoples postures and body languages in whole. As I mentioned before do we have many cultures in this world. What seems "this way" in one culture might be interpret completely different in another. You know: "this way" here, and "that way" there, so make sure to have the cultural differences in mind while speaking to different people. This out of respect. Apart from the cultural differences that we have to bear in mind, we also need to be aware of the differences *within* a specific culture. This said, a person *might* interpret different behaviors, completely dependent on the situation. So be aware and have respect toward everyone!

204

"Communication – the human connection – is the key to personal and career success" – Paul J. Meyer.

HOW TO SPEAK IN FRONT OF PEOPLE

To make my point, I will start of this part of the chapter by giving you two scenarios. After these two scenarios, I am going to ask you a question, and then we will continue with how you best can influence the people in your surrounding.

Scenario 1: You are in a seminar where a person suddenly appears in the spotlight. You think to yourself: "Here we go!" You prepare yourself with a peace of paper and your favourite pen. The person enters with a great smile. Even though you do not see her fully, you sense the aura she brings. She almost fluids in – with a walking compared to a butterfly: so beautiful. Her hands are shown, where she waves at you, and you think to yourself: "I swear, that hello was meant for me". She continues to the point in the scene where she will stand. There, she finds herself looking around, where you now feel interested. She had made an impression on you – the friendly one. Her smile, that walk, and that wave all said something to you, did they not? What this lady was aiming for was being friendly before start talking – to loosen you up. And now you are wondering: "I wonder what she'll start of with". The topic you are aware off, otherwise you would not be there. It is your favourite topic – you live for this. She looks around and then opens her mouth. Throughout the seminar, she interacts with the audience, making sure to answer bodily expressions that signal questions. Up there, she looks around and whenever she feels like you need interactions, she makes sure to crack a joke or ask something. She does this to get your fully attention, and this by showing her fully potential. Her intention is for you to go home with one thing in your mind and that is: being more passionate about this topic than before. She wants to give you more fuel. And you can sense this. Her energy spots her intention away, where you, throughout the seminar, see her having an open body language. Her vocal chords changes, this so you can follow when there is something more to pitch at, or when she is getting herself into a complete different character. This woman on stage really knows what she is talking about, do she not? From her posture to her gestures, from her expressions to her movements on the stage. She has mastered the knowledge on how to communicate in the best way – in a way that she comes across to you. And when the seminar comes to an end, she ends it beautifully with an epic "thinker". And then she says goodbye and walks, like a butterfly, out of the stage. At this point, you are nothing but happy. This woman has taught you a lot, has she not? She have given you examples to aspects you already knew, but she gave you a different point of view too; she gave you information you never knew before. And she gave you a conversation you will never forget. Because one thing you need to have in mind: these people focus on

206

dialog rather than a monolog. This is primarily done by talking and then asking, and then talking again. These people focus on interactions *with* you – rather than speaking *to* you. These people make sure to be one of you – not above you. And most importantly: they make you aware. So in the end you are really fired up about this, are you not?

Scenario 2: You are in the same seminar, but a different personality appears. The person who appears on stage wraps herself towards the middle, where she, up to this point, has not shown any open body language. You can sense by her aura that she is shy, or maybe afraid. Or is it insecurity? Either way, that sense you got gave you uncertainty as well, did it not? Now you think to yourself: "Why is she so shy and insecure for? I mean, does she not want to be here? Is she maybe forced to do these kind of events?" As you can sense in the room, you are not the only one having these thoughts, are you? And as a result, the whole room have dark clouds over it – the cloud I would like to call: the negative aura. By this point, you already made up your mind about her. Clearly she did not want to be here, so why would you? This makes you uninterested, and by that thought, your body shuts off. You fold yourself. Throughout the seminar, you stay the same way – folid. It does not matter what she knows and how much she can teach you – she clearly has not mastered how to give that information to you. She does not come through that negative aura she caused. You find yourself dazzling of to thoughts such as "What to eat?", "How are my children/friends/family/pets doing?", "I wonder if I should watch how to get away with murder later?[18]". Suddenly the seminar has come to an end. When the person on stage says: "Now we have time for questions", you have realized that this woman on stage has nothing else but been talking for a whole hour, without having any interactions with the people in the room. You really do not like this woman, do you? Something within you says that she thinks that she is inferior to you – and you do not like it at all. Looking around, you see people reacting in the way that you do. What is this woman doing? Clearly she is not a successful lady, is she? I mean, you could have done that better than her, could you not? And do not fight me on this. I know that you have been in a room where you have thought this exact thought. When she walks off, you realize that no one made effort to ask question, but you already know why. She did not make any effort – so why would you? And when she leaves, you have this clouds surrounding you. It is called "guilt". Now you feel empathy for her. "Maybe she was just too shy?", "Maybe this was her first time and here we were, giving her a hard time?" And there you go, drowning yourself in destruct toward you own bad behaviours.

---

[18] *How to get away with murder is a TV-series created by Peter Nowalk.*

What is the difference between these two scenarios I just gave you? – Reading this far, I bet you screamed: "It is all about having an open dialog with the opponent". Was I right? –Correct! You are really becoming your own success and I could nothing but be happy for you. The reason I gave you these two scenarios is to make you aware of the fact that what we express is far more precious than what we say verbally. This said, people who have mastered the way to interact in the successful way could make any topic interesting. Even math. Therefore, knowing how to talk to an audience is a must to be able to influence in the way you want to. I have had stage fright, which means that I was not a fan of talking in front of a big audience. This is something that I have had as an anxiety since I was a child, and it all comes from me being extremely insecure and shy as a child. I did not want to be seen and therefore hated to be in the centre of attention. That meant judgements and judgement meant lack of acceptance. I could not take more than what I already had gotten. So I focused on being silent and usually "behind-the-curtains-kind-of-girl", to protect me from others physical and verbal acts. However, during my years at the University, I started to tackle this fright and this was mainly done by mastering my own mind. See, you can make yourself think what you want yourself to believe. This by switching views. I knew that, but I also knew that the brain needed to be taken care of beforehand so what I did was that I found the reasons for my anxiety and mastered those fears one by one. And then I visualized towards success. Yet, I still have some stage fright, but not in the same amount. I just get nervous the first 2-5 minutes and then live every minute left of it. *How?* – I mastered my mind into knowing how to communicate with people, whether it is an audience of 1, 10, 100 or 10 000. I made sure to deal with my inside, and then work towards visualizing myself succeeding on that stage. To make a correlation to scenario 2 above, I would like to mention that the woman on stage could be one of these women, the ones that have stage fright. Maybe she has been judged wrongly before. Maybe this was her way of dealing with that fear, who knows? This is not something you can read on a person. And this is also why it is important to deal with your closet beforehand. Even if you have stage fright, you need to be able to know how to interact in the best way, and maybe even say something that goes: "I'm sorry if I come across as arrogant or shut off, but I am mastering my stage fright so bear with me." Solely this sentence will make people in your surrounding go more easy on you – this because you made them aware, and made them have empathy for you. Transparency. That was the difference to the scenario I painted in scenario 2; she simply did not make you aware of why she shut you out. That is also why you judged her actions. We simply judge by what we see. If you do not communicate why and that *why* cannot be answered, you will fail. This is something that is imprinted in us. We do not do it to hurt people; we do this to try to understand people. And yes, sometimes we can judge wrongly, but that is also the reason why we need to make sure to not give any signals that can be interpreted wrongly. This further shows the importance of verbal communication. We cannot read minds – which is why you need to make the people in your surrounding aware of why you are shut off in different occasions. This will make them go easy on you – and make you go easy on yourself.

By this said, you need to increase your knowledge in how to speak properly in a crowd, in front of an audience or just by yourself talking to yourself in the mirror. The way you speak is influenced by your thinking and confidence. This said, *what* you say is influenced by your body language. If you are uncertain about a thing you just have spoken, usually your uncertainty is shown in your body language. Our body language acts after our feelings, which is controlled by our subconscious. This means that our body shows us what we feel inside, which can either support or contradict to what you just said verbally. This basically means that you give away yourself if you lie, and since words can be manipulated do we tend to believe a person's non-verbal cues. We cannot control our body language (well to some extent we can), but we can be aware of it by knowing ourselves better. By getting to know ourselves more, we tend to know how we feel, and therefore observe both our body movements and the peoples' in our surrounding. So my advice to you is: speak up when you are right about a thing and can protect that statement, and if you cannot, ask questions instead. Why? Because your body language will signal doubt if you give a statement on something you have neither awareness nor confidence in. To become a successful lady you need to communicate in A-style. A-style means communicate with knowledge in every sentence you speak, since you need to know what you actually are saying and standing for or against. Foremost, A-style also means speaking with style. It is therefore important for your body language to be correlated with your talking. Always have in mind to never utter something that will upset another human being. Manners ladies! Always be aware of *what* you are saying, *why* you are saying it, *where* you are saying it and *how* you are saying it. It all needs to be well formulated so no one can give you accusations. A-style, ladies. A-style!

Something else to bear in mind is that everything you feel is communicated from the inside out, which is the reason why I am telling you to focus more on the inside. The more you know about your self and your pros and cons, the more we can focus on your advantages and therefore shine in those areas. Additionally is it good to know what your feelings are in this moment, since it will be communicated by your body language. Example, you are afraid of dogs and therefore will be scared whenever you see one. What signals will this act give the surrounding I might ask you? Another example is when we are on a date and we like the person and the feelings are mutual, what do the people in our

212

surrounding see? What do we radiate with our bodies? Yes, you are right! It all starts and ends in the brain, where mental knowledge is something I cannot stress enough about. Also bear in mind that some actions or behaviours we have are hidden to us (as we have mentioned before). We are not aware of them. Therefore is my advice to you to ask people in your surroundings about **flaws** they noticed in you. I always try to do this. And ladies, take the critique as positively as you can. You have to remember that it might not have been easy for the other person to utter these acknowledgements to you. Also, the person made you a favour. Now you will be able to be aware and focus on those critiques, which as a result will end up with you changing those bad ones to better ones instead. That is why you need to thank the person who is giving you critique as warmly as you can.

This is a great time to move to the last sub-headline of this headline, namely the branding. Since you now are aware of your thinking, your behaviour, your actions, and your non-verbal communication – it is time to put it all into action in form of branding yourself.

BRANDNIG

You brand yourself all the time, whether you like it or not. Branding is even done by only stepping outside the door. You might not think that you brand yourself but look at it this way: *Do people see you when you go outside?* The true answer is that at least one person sees you when you step outdoors, which will make you a target of judgments. And do not get mad at them for doing it: that is human nature. We are programmed to judge the book by its cover. This is how we survived in cave years: is this person a friend, a foe, or a potential partner? But to you I say: be the better person and stop judging others as much as you can. Stop with labelling from previous prejudices and stereotyping and start judging from experiences instead. But, to make this possible, you need to change your state of mind if you want to be the person you dream of (as we have highlighted at least a thousand times throughout this book). Once we change that thinking-pattern and judging of yours, we can focus on what really matters; your inside out. Because one thing you need to have in mind: *what you want people too see comes from within.* As I have mentioned already, we need to get our inside to match with our outside, which is done by changing the inside first. If you have great clothing and you have this selfish behaviour – but you are trying to cover your selfishness by being like a loving and carrying person – people are going to see right thru you and that cover of yours. And you know what happens then? Your branding becomes just that, false and completely destroyed by that occasion. With this statement I want to highlight *footprint.* Footprint in this occasion means to live the way you want to be remembered for. This way you will not be acting like a person with two faces but you will actually start living the way you want others to see you as. This way you will get rid of your false

214

facades and masks as well. Remember, you first need to convince yourself in order to convince others. We want your branding to be nothing short of spectacular, which includes a lot of looking-into-what-I-have-to-say-and-follow-my-steps-in-these-chapters-toward-your-success, lady!

All and all, to be able to influence your branding in the best way possible, you need to use communication to your advantage. Your emotions are reflected and therefore communicated in the way you move, so use this wisely. By using non-verbal communication to your advantage, you will be able to mirror the other person, as well as talking about a subject they love. Mirroring is when you copy the other person's reflections, which sends out signals that you admire or like the other person. By making the other person mirror you, you fully know that her attention is on you. By mirroring others, it shows the other person that you listen and hear what she is talking about. For example: your friend has been on a trip with her boyfriend and wants to tell you all about it. By mirroring her words – simply by repeating the last word she says (called probbing) – you will give the impression of interest. This will result in her telling her story with more enthusiasm since she now knows that you are interested. Furthermore could you interpret with sentences such as: "You have mentioned just a second ago…", "You have just said that you didn't like…" or things that will give away the expression that you actually was listening to her. And ladies, please, these sentences can be seen through if you do not listen to her. Therefore, use them wisely. Furthermore could you also mirror the facial expression she uses when she talks. This will show her that you are listening carefully. And my best advice to you is: nod! Whenever she is talking, nod as a notification that you have heard everything she told you and that she can keep going. This nod will not only signal that you agree of what she tells you, but that you follow the story as well. Always bear in mind the golden rule: how would you have wanted to be approached when talking? Behave that way yourself! This way, the opponent will start liking you more without even realizing why. The reason is simple: we like people who are like us. In this way, by mirroring as well as talking about their favourite topic, you have used communication to your advantage. This is called "the chameleon effect[19]" simply because we mirror our environment. Businessmen and businesswomen use this method all the time. As the business people are using their communication to their branding, you are doing the same. As mentioned a thousand times in this book: start with yourself, and work yourself out. Make yourself believe in you before you let others to.

---

[19] *Applies when an interaction between two people goes well, where both of them use mirroring or mimics of the other person's non-verbal communication. The chameleon effect is confirmed by experiments, such as the Chartrand and Bargh experiments.*

You see me walking down the street – all caught up in the music played from my phone. You see me walking by and I do not even notice that you are looking at me. Do you like what you see? Picture me walking down the streets of Stockholm, with a walk that will take your breath away. How can she be so confident, you might ask yourself. You keep on looking at me and find my walk elegant and you almost envy the way I move myself, almost in contrast to the butterflies in the air. However, by now you should already know the answer to your own question. I have mastered the skill to communicate with my brain. I have also mastered the skill to know my self, and therefore, how to behave in certain ways to make sure I am giving my point across. Yes, what you envy is how confident I look and that my self-confidence is showed in the walk, as well as in my dressing. Until now you have not even realized what I was wearing. You were too busy with noticing my confidence and that is exactly how it all works. Confidence permeates everything. You like what you see. But, here is the thing. What you see is not only me. What you see is yourself too. This image I just portrayed in your brain is you as well. This is how far you have come. You have mastered the "think", "behavior", "act" and "talk" of a true successful lady. You have worked on the inside, and now it is time to focus on your last puzzle bite of your cover: namely the conclusion of all. So, let us do just that. Let us dig into that part of the outside.

As I end this last chapter, before diving into the "conclusion"-part, I want you to take a moment and just reflect. Reflect on everything you have just read. Everything. From the very first day: when you bought this book, until this very moment: as you are reading these sentences. *Have your life changed? Are you seeing the world differently? Are you seeing yourself differently? What are your feelings? Excitement? Nervous? Happiness? What are your thoughts? Is this what you predicted all along?* But most importantly: ***Have I convinced you?*** *Have I convinced you into believing in yourself? Have I convinced you that you have what it takes? And have I convinced you that you are worth the life you dream of? Once again: have I convinced you?*

And as you answer these questions honestly, I want you to refer back to this journey we have just made. Now you possess valuable information and knowledge. Make sure to use it well. For greater and for good. I am looking forward to see you out there, true successful lady!

"The only thing that's keeping you from getting what you want is the story you keep telling yourself" – Tony Robbins.

By adding to this quote by one of my biggest role models, I want to make sure you communicate positively with your brain: belief, confidence and positive thinking towards self-development and self-respect.

218

Look yourself in the mirror. Look yourself in the window a dark evening. Look at what the reflection shows in that moment. Take any given moment you become aware. Just look at yourself. What are your thoughts and beliefs in that moment – and how do those thoughts and beliefs influence your non-verbal and verbal communication? Make sure to be aware. Make sure to catch yourself in bad patterns, to be able to change them toward better ones for your inside and outside. To be able to have a great talk and walk, you need to look within to be able to see how your outside is influenced by your emotions, feelings, thoughts and beliefs. Be aware future successful lady. Be aware of how your gestures, postures, facial expressions and bodily movements in general get influenced by your inside. Therefore, look at the reflection of you passing by a building. Do you like what you see? Do that lady walking by – looking at you at the exact time as you look at her – express whatever you want to see in yourself?

PART 4

WALKING UP THE VISION LANE

As a Conclusion, I want to give you a last motivation:

One last thought to our future successful ladies out there. By changing your life, you will be changing the history and the lives of our future daughters.

One thing I have realized, which probably will not make me the only one, is that all the people we bring up into consideration as legends or role models within business and other areas are men. How many of them are actually women? Well, Oprah Winfrey and Serena Williams are mentioned from time to time. But what about Sara Blakely – the founder and owner of Spanx? What about Sheryl Sandberg, who has been Facebook's COO since 2008 and was the first woman in Facebook's board? And what about the CEO of Burberry, namely Ahrendts?

I oftentimes hear names such as Elon Musk, Warren Buffett, Steve Jobs, Bill Gates, Mark Zuckerberg, Jeff Bezos, Jack Ma, Walt Disney, Sergey Brinn and Larry Page. What do all these people in common? – They are all men. A notification: I do not mean to bring them up as negativity, absolutely not. In fact, I admire each and one of them for their differences and willingness to fight for what they desire and believe. However, I brought them up to get my point across, and to make the ladies realize that they can be one of the future role models as well.

There is no surprise that women have had more obstacles facing them during their way to a successful life. However, it is our destiny to do something about the current state we are in. To change the rules in our own minds. To play chess with the same power as the queen has. Simply put, to own the game!

What I want to highlight with this book is for you to aim for what you want. Ladies shall be able to aim high, and land higher if they wish. They also need to make a mark simply by focusing on bigger goals than the ones they have today. We ladies need to constantly improve ourselves. We need to constantly develop and give more to this world. Ladies today have ambitions and goals, which also needs to be satisfied in any way. Make sure to reach your goals and keep aiming higher! In today's society we have possibilities, which is constantly in progress towards the better. Therefore, make sure to take advantage of them. We are fortunate enough to have the ability to do what we put our minds to, as long as we put our thoughts, beliefs, focus and heart into it. But most importantly, by never giving up. Because let us be honest, women might have a harder way towards reaching the top, in comparison to men. Instead of this tearing us down, it should give us the motivation to start as earlier as possible so we get ahead of the game. With other words, we need to see it from a whole different angle and not see the negativity in it – but the opportunity and reward instead. We simply need to fight harder since it will be something that will be rewarded in the future, when you stand there as a Victorian, where you have taught yourself a lot about the competitors and the market in your unique area. Additionally, throughout this fight will you also learn what the others expect from you, as well as what you expect from both them and yourself. This is something my sister and me taught ourselves in a young age simply because our surname was not (and is not) "Swedish". This was my first acquaintance with Mr. Discrimination and from the age of six, I walked a road of discrimination – both from the environment as well as from myself. This first discrimination made some teachers and peers judge us by this specific surname and not our capacity. This (in turn) made us fight 300% more than we did before, simply to prove them wrong. Even though we got taught from our parents that the road would get tough, we kept on walking a walk based on grenades. But we managed to get through – we managed to become the ones we wanted to be all along.

"Never judge the person by her name. The name never shows her true potential. What's inside is only shown by actions and behaviors so if you need to judge something, judge that. Judge a person's actions and behaviors instead. Those actions and behaviors will lead to success and branding, and by then, her name will be something bigger than herself. So, never judge the person by her name. You will end up adoring her name in the end".

By deciding to focus on you and your dreams, you will be able to be a part of this development toward a better world for all the ladies. All the ladies out there that have lost themselves in any way. Simply by developing yourself to the better version of you, you will develop your thoughts as well, which will impact another lady's thoughts too. This will start a chain reaction so make sure you take a part of this reaction – it will be a trend you will grow and glow in. A trend that will influence your daughter in a positive way!

Let the chain reaction begin – it all begins with you and me, together, taking a stand towards the future. It all starts with transparency and interdependence. A step closer towards what will be the change of your future toward the better one. It all starts with a few people taking the matter into their own hands and them making sure to be the helping hand our future desperately cries for. To be the help for the future ladies out there and to stand for courage; for making changes they want in their lives – changes that will make ladies accept their destiny and not drawback from any setbacks coming in their ways. We make sure to not only fight for our own future, but for all the other ladies as well. It all starts with us –interdepending on one another – stepping up and show our abilities and that we matter too, and it all ends with success within us. We are all equal, and shall be treated equally, no matter the gender identity, color of your skin, shape of your body, culture or profession. Always remember: small changes will lead to bigger ones in the future.

226

A butterfly's movement in Brazil will lead to hurricanes in Mexico – the butterfly effect[20]. So, make sure to start the butterfly effect, whether you are located in Europe, Asia, America, Australia, Africa or Oceania, because it will affect other ladies as well. Let the TSL-organization start the future of a unified front: a united front towards self-respect and interdependence in one another. A united front I wish I had as a past.

"Nothing could delight me more than to see the woman taking up her distinctive position in society. Nothing should hinder her progress. Like men, women deserve the right to occupy high positions according to their capabilities and qualifications."
– The Founding Father of UAE, Sheikh Zayed bin Sultan Al Nahyan
(may Almighty Allah rest his soul in peace)

I hope you will find this book and the TSL-organization useful and an organization to lean against whenever you will need some support. As I have mentioned before, I have been walking the same unfortunate road, which is the reason why I want to help you get through yours, the way my better half helped me out from mine. I end this book my saying:

---

[20] *A phenomenon that shows that a small change in a specific place will have a major change in another place.*

"Age is just a number and sex is just a gender identity. It is what is in your brain that matters – and more importantly, what you do with it. So start learning as much as you can because the more knowledge you have, the more success you will have, for the very reason that the more you know, the more things will you be able to handle yourself."

\- Yours truly, the founders of the TSL-organization.

REFERENCES:

Articles and books:

Aesop. (1781). *Fables of Æsop and others [Elektronisk resurs]: Translated into English. With morals and instructive applications, and a print before each fable. To which is prefixed, the life of Æsop, more enlarged than in any former edition of this size.* Aberdeen: Printed and sold by James Chalmers and Co..

Ahrne, G. & Svensson, P. (2015). Handbok I kvalitativa metoder. 2:2 upplagan. Stockholm: Liber AB.

Amaya, K., Bruderlin, A & Calvert, T. (1996). Emotion from Motion. In Graphic Interface, 222-229.

Aronoff, J., Woike, B. A. & Hyman, L. M. (1992). Which Are the Stimuli in Facial Displays of anger and happiness? Configurationl bases of emotion recognition. *Journal of Personality and Social Psychology*, 62 (6): 1050-1066.

Bandura, A. (1995). *Self-Efficacy in Changing Societies.* New York: Cambridge UP, Print.

Bauman, Z. & May, T. (2004). *Att tänka sociologiskt.* Upplaga 2:a omarbetade upplagan. Göteborg.

Benabou, R. & Tirole, J. (2000). *Self-confidence and social interactions.* Cambridge, Mass.: National Bureau of Economic Research.

Bernard, L. L. (1926). "Behavior Patterns: Their Nature and Development." Chapter 8 in *An Introduction to Social Psychology.* New York: Henry Holt and Co: 106-122.

Bickhard, M. H., Christopher, J. C. (manuscript, 1989) The Influence of Early Experience on Personality Development.

Bolman, L.G & Deal, T.E (2012), *Nya perspektiv på organisation och ledarskap.* Pozkal, Polen 2012.

Brown, S. & Smith, D. (2006). *Active listening. [Student's book]. 1.* (2. ed.) Cambridge: Cambridge University Press.

Byrne, R. (2007). *The secret*. Energica.

Catania, A.C., Harnad, S. & Skinner, B.F. (red.) (1988). *The selection of behavior: the operant behaviorism of B.F. Skinner : comments and consequences*. Cambridge: Cambridge U.P.

Chartrand, T.L., Bargh, J.A. (1999) The Chameleon Effect: The Perception-Behavior Link and Social Interaction. *Journal of Personality and Social Psychology*. 1999, Vol. 76, 893-910.

Cialdini, R.B. (1993). *Influence: the psychology of persuasion*. (Rev. ed.) New York, NY: Morrow.

Collins, J.C. (2001). *Good to great: why some companies make the leap- and others don't*. (1st ed.) New York, NY: HarperBusiness.

Cannon, W.B. (1929). *Bodily changes in pain, hunger, fear and rage: an account of recent researches into the function of emotional excitement*. (2d ed.) New York: D. Appleton and Company.

Covey, S.R. (2005). *The 7 habits of highly effective people: personal workbook*. London: Simon & Schuster.

Coverman, S. (1989). Role overload, role conflict, and stress: Addressing consequences of multiple role demands. *Social Forces*, *67*(4), 965–982.

Darwin, Charles. 1872. *The Expression of the Emotions in Man and Animals*. Oxford University Press. USA.

Dillon, R.S. (1997) Self-Respect: Moral, Emotional, Political. *An International Journal of Social, Political, and legal Philosophy*. Volume 107, no. 2., 226-249.

Dispenza, F. (2017). *Becoming supernatural - how common people are doing the uncommon*. Hay House Inc.

Dispenza, J. (2014). *You are the placebo: making your mind matter*. Carlsbad, California: Hay House, Inc..

Downey, B. (2015). The Looking Glass self and Deliberation Bias in Qualitative Interviews. *Sociological Spectrum*, 35 (6); 534-551.

Dunne, L. (2017). *Lagom: the Swedish art of balanced living*. London: Gaia.

Edelstein, M., Brant, D., Rouw, R. & Ramachandran, V. S. (2013). Misophonia: Physiological investigations and case descriptions. *Frontiers in human neuroscience*, (7) 296.

Eklund, F. & Littlefield, B. (2015). *Sälj!: konsten att sälja vad som helst till vem som helst.* Stockholm: Ekerlid.

Ekman, P. (red.) (1982). *Emotion in the human face.* (2., [rev.] ed.) Cambridge: Cambridge U. P

Ekman, Paul, and Wallace V. Friesen. 1967. "Head and Body Cues in the Judgment of Emotion: A Reformulation." Perceptual and Motor Skills 24 (3): 711–724.

Eksvärd, E. (2015). *Vardagsmakt.* [Stockholm]: Månpocket.

Fast, J. (1970). *Body language.* New York: M. Evans; distributed in association with Lippincott.

Floyd, K. (2014). Communication matters. (2. ed.) New York: McGraw-Hill.

Forslund, M. (2009). *Organisation och ledning.* 1st edition. Elanders, Sverige.

Freud, A. (1937). *The ego and the mechanisms of defence.* London: Hogarth Press.

Frosh, S. (1991). *Identity crisis: modernity, psychoanalysis and the self.* London: Macmillan.

Giddens, A. Sutton, P. (2013) *Sociologi.* Lund: Studentlitteratur.

Goman, C.K. (2008). *The nonverbal advantage [Elektronisk resurs] secrets and science of body language at work.* San Francisco, Calif.: Berrett-Koehler.

Hansen, A. (2016). *Hjärnstark. [Elektronisk resurs] : hur motion och träning stärker din hjärna.* Fitnessförlaget.

Harrigan, J.A., Rosenthal, R. & Scherer, K.R. (red.) (2005). *The new handbook of methods in nonverbal behavior research.* New York: Oxford University Press.

Hashim IH, Zhiliang Y. (2003). Cultural and gender differences in perceiving stressors: A cross-cultural investigation of African and Western students in Chinese colleges. *Stress Health*, 19, 217–225.

Hill, N. (2008). *Think and Grow Rich.* Wilder Publications.

Hokanson, J. E., Burgess, M., & Cohen, M.F. (1963) Effects of displaced aggression on systolic blood pressure. *Journal of Abnormal and Social Psychology,* 67, 214-218.

Holt, N. (2012). *Psychology: the science of mind and behaviour.* (2., [rev., European] ed.) Maidenhead: McGraw-Hill Higher Education.

Hunt, M.G., Marx, Rachel., Lipson, C. & Young, J. (2018). No More FOMO: Limiting Social Media Decreases Loneliness and Depression. *Journal of Social and Clinical Psychology*: Vol. 37, No. 10, pp. 751-768.

Irwin, L. G., Siddiqi, A. & Hertzman, C. (2007). Early Child Development: A Powerful Equalizer. Final Report for the World Health Organization's Commission on the Social Determinants of Health

Jenkins, R. (2008). *Social identity.* (3. ed.) London: Routledge.

Johansson, T. & Lalander, P. (2013). *Vardagslivets socialpsykologi.* (2., [utök. och uppdaterade] uppl.) Stockholm: Liber.

Johnson. C. E. (2015) *Meeting the Ethical Challenges of Leadership*, Sage publications, London, 5th edition.

Kahneman, D. (2013). *Thinking, fast and slow.* (1st pbk. ed.) New York: Farrar, Straus and Giroux.

Kaufmann, G & Kaufmann, A (2010). *Psykologi i organisation och ledning.* Dimograf, Polen 2014.

Ketchen, D and Short, J. (2016). *Mastering Strategic Management.* Edition 2016. Published under a Creative commons (CC BY-NC-SA) license.

Kidder, D. L. (2002). The influence of gender on the performance of organizational citizenship behaviors. *Journal of management*, 28(5), 629–648.

Kim, S. M., Han, D. H., Trksak, G. H., & Lee, Y (2013). Gender differences in Adolescent coping behaviours and suicidal ideation: Findings from a sample of 73,238 adolescents. *Suicide and Life-Threatening Behaviour,* 45 (4), 477-487.

Kotler, P., Armstrong, G., Harris, C.H. & Piercy, N. (2016). Principals of marketing: European Edition. Edition 6. Pearson Education Limited.

Kroger, J. (1996). *Identity in adolescence: the balance between self and other.* (2. ed.) London: Routledge.

Lawrence, J., Ashford, K., Dent, P (2006). Gender differences in coping strategies of Undergraduate students and their impact on self-esteem and attention. *Active Learning in Higher Education,* 3, 273-281.

Lazarus, R.S. & Folkman, S. (1984). *Stress, appraisal, and coping* (1st ed.). New York: Springer.

Leaf, C. (2017). *Switch on your brain: the key to peak happiness, thinking and health Workbook.* Grand Rapids, Michigan: Baker Publishing Group.

Lipton, B.H. (2015). *The biology of belief: unleashing the power of consciousness, matter and miracles.* (2015, 10th anniversary edition). Carlsbad, CA: Hay House

Lipton, B. (2014). *Honeymoon effect - the science of creating heaven on earth.* Hay House UK Ltd

Locke, J. (1976[1977]). *An essay concerning human understanding.* (New ed., abridged). London: Dent.

Lurie, A. (1981). *The language of clothes.* New York: Random House.

Mack, J. (2002) Karma 101: *What goes around comes around ... and what you can do about it.* Fair Winds Press.

Mehrabian, A. (1972). *Silent messages.* Belmont, Calif.

Mehrabian, A. (1981). *Silent messages: implicit communication of emotions and attitudes.* (2. ed.) Belmont, Calif.: Wadsworth.

Mckay, M. (2009). *Messages: the communication skills book - the communication skills book.* New Harbinger Publications,u.s.

McSweeney, F.K. & Murphy, E.S. (2014). *The Wiley-Blackwell Handbook of Operant and Classical Conditioning [Elektronisk resurs].* Wiley.

Meyer, J. (2016). *The mind connection: how the thoughts you choose affect your mood, behavior, and decisions.* (1. trade paperback ed.) New York: FaithWords.

Navarro, J. (2008). *What every body is saying: an ex-FBI agent's guide to speed reading people*. (1. ed.) New York, NY: Collins.

Peale, N.V. (1998[1953]). *The power of positive thinking*. London: Vermilion.

Pease, A.Pease, A. (2014). *Body language*. Manjul Publishing House Pvt Lt.

Pease, A. & Pease, B. (2006). *The definitive book of body language*. (Bantam hardcover ed.) New York: Bantam Books.

Pineda, J.A. (red.) (2009). *Mirror neuron systems: the role of mirroring processes in social cognition*. New York: Humana.

Poyatos, F. (2001). *Nonverbal communication across disciplines. Vol. 2, Paralanguage, kinesics, silence, personal and environmental interaction*. Amsterdam: J. Benjamins Pub. Co..

Rachlin, H. (1979). Review of Classical conditioning and operant conditioning: A response pattern analysis. Psyccritiques. 24(7): 579-597.

Robbins, A. (1991). *Awaken the giant within: how to take immediate control of your mental, emotional, physical & financial destiny*. New York, N.Y.: Summit Books.

Robinson, J.P., Shaver, P.R., Wrightsman, L.S. & Andrews, F.M. (red.) (1991). *Measures of personality and social psychological attitudes*. San Diego: Academic Press.

Rogers, C.R. (1974[1967]). *On becoming a person: a therapist's view of psychotherapy*. ([New ed.], repr.) London: Constable.

Saklofske, H. Austin, E. Mastoras, S. Beaton, L. Osborne, S., (2012). Relationships of personality, affect, emotional intelligence and coping with student stress and academic success: Different patterns of association for stress and success. *ScienceDirect*, 22, 251-257.

Simonson, N. (2009). *Varför mår vi så dåligt när vi har det så bra?*. Bonnier Audio.

Sinek, S. (2009). *Start with why: how great leaders inspire everyone to take action*. London: Portfolio Penguin.

Sinek, S. (2017). *Leaders eat last: why some teams pull together and others don't*. London: Penguin Books Ltd.

Skinner, B.F (1953). *Science and human behavior.* New York: Macmillian.

Skinner, B.F. (1954) The science of learning and the art of teaching. *Harvard Educational Review,* 24(2), 86-97.

Solomon, M. (2016). *Consumer behaviour: a European perspective.* 6 ed. Harlow: Pearson.

Stewart, C.J. & Cash, W.B. (1999). Interviewing: principles and practices. (9. ed.) Boston: McGraw-Hill College.

Sun, T. (2008). *The art of war Art of war.* Penguin Books Ltd.

Sung, J. & Hanna, S (1996). Factors related to risk tolerance. *Finance counselling and planning,* Vo. 7. Sverige. Bibelkommissionen (1973) (1999). *Bibeln.* Örebro: Libris.

Trew, K., & Kremer, J. (1998). *Gender & Psychology.* 1st Ed. Arnold, London.

Trost, J. (2010). *Kvalitativa intervjuer.* Lund: Studentlitteratur AB.

Vosk, Barbara N., Rex Forehand, and Rolando Figueroa. 1983. "Perception of Emotions by Accepted and Rejected Children." *Journal of Behavioral Assessment* 5 (2): 151–160.

Walton, D.C. (2015). *Caveman rules of survival - 3 simple rules used by our brains to keep us sa.* John Hunt Publishing.

Watson, J.B. (1970) Behaviorism. New York: Norton.

Westman, M. (2006). Crossover of stress and strain in the work-family context. In F. Jones, R. J. Burke, & M. Westman (Eds.), *Work-life balance: A psychological perspective* (pp. 163-184). New York, NY, US: Psychology Press.

Wood, M, J. (2015). Eliminating Fear: How Removing the Fear of God Leads to Removing Fear in Life. *The Destiny Hub Press.*

Yeung, K-T., & Martin, J, L. (2003). The Looking Glass Self: An Empirical Test and Elaboration. *Social Forces,* 81 (3); 843-879.

Videos:

Avicii (2013) Avicii – Wake me up (Official Video). From: https://www.youtube.com/watch?v=IcrbM1l_BoI (2019-02-07)

Be inspired (2018). "THE 1%" ARE DOING THIS EVERYDAY | Reprogram Your Subconscious Mind | Try It For 21 Days! From: https://www.youtube.com/watch?v=hv1k2YG0JK8 (2019-01-14).

David Crossman (2016) Simon Sinek on Millennials in the Workplace. From: https://www.youtube.com/watch?v=hER0Qp6QJNU (2019-02-07)

Law of Attraction Coaching (2018). Tony Robbins: How to Become More Disciplined (MUST WATCH). From: https://www.youtube.com/watch?v=SBgKfFX3uZE (2019-01-14).

London Real (2016). HOW TO REPROGRAM YOUR SUBCONSCIOUS - Dandapani on London Real. From: https://www.youtube.com/watch?v=Gku2OodrnQ0 (2019-01-14).

Mathemate Videos (2016) A world where fish are no longer forced to climb trees. From: https://www.youtube.com/watch?v=paVkw5ZmsG4(2019-02-07)

Michael Jackson (2010) Michael Jackson – In the closet (Official Video). From: https://www.youtube.com/watch?v=4qLY0vbrT8Q (2019-02-07)

No1potterhead (2014) The Original Harry Potter ScreenTest that started it all – Daniel Radcliffe (Harry). From: https://www.youtube.com/watch?v=7WqhS5o52T4 (2019-02-07)

Other Live (2017). Tony Robbins: How To Master Your Emotions (Tony Robbins Psychology). From: https://www.youtube.com/watch?v=agw4pKG880Q (2019-01-14).

OWN (2011) What Oprah learned from Jim Carrey | Oprah's Life Class | Oprah Winfrey Network. From: https://www.youtube.com/watch?v=nPU5bjzLZX0 (2019-02-07)

OWN (2017). Gary Zukav: The New Perception of Community with Oprah Winfrey | SuperSoul Sessions | OWN. From: https://www.youtube.com/watch?v=OJ6okNOxRqo (2019-01-13).

Sinek, S. (2016). The Millennial Question. From: https://www.youtube.com/watch?v=vudaAYx2IcE (2019-01-14).

TED (2010) How great leaders inspire action | Simon Sinek. From: https://www.youtube.com/watch?v=qp0HIF3Sfl4 (2019-02-07)

TED (2007). Why we do what we do | Tony Robbins. From: https://www.youtube.com/watch?v=Cpc-t-Uwv1I (2019-01-14).

TED (2012) Your body language may shape who you are. From: https://www.youtube.com/watch?v=Ks-_Mh1QhMc&t=88s (2019-02-08)

TEDx Talks (2016) Unwavering Focus | Dandapani | TEDxReno. From: https://www.youtube.com/watch?v=4O2JK_94g3Y (2019-02-07)

TEDx Talks (2011) TEDxMaastricht – Simon Sinek – "First why and then trust". From: https://www.youtube.com/watch?v=4VdO7LuoBzM (2019-02-07)

TedxTalks (2013). The importance of Being Inauthentic: Marc Bowden at TEDxToronto. From: https://www.youtube.com/watch?v=1zpf8H_Dd40&t=2s (2019-01-13).

TedxTalks (2015). To reach beyond your limits by training your mind | Marisa Peer | TEDxKCS. From: https://www.youtube.com/watch?v=zCv-ZBy6_yU (2019-01-14).

TedxTalks (2016). Body Language: The Key to Your Subconscious | Ann Washburn | TEDxIdahoFalls. From: https://www.youtube.com/watch?v=_v36Vt9GmH8 (2019-01-14).

TedxTalks (2016). The Caveman rules of survival | Dawn Walton | TEDxDundee. From: https://www.youtube.com/watch?v=Dv543zNEvGE (2019-01-14).

TedxTalks (2017). You are contagious | Vanessa Van Edwards | TEDxLondon. From: https://www.youtube.com/watch?v=cef35Fk7YD8 (2019-01-22).

The Little Albert Experiment (2010). From: https://www.youtube.com/watch?v=9hBfnXACsOI (2019-01-13)

Tom Bilyeu (2018) How to unlock the Full Potential of Your Mind | Dr. Joe Dispenza on Impact Theory. From: https://www.youtube.com/watch?v=La9oLLoI5Rc (2019-02-07)

World Porn (2018). How to NEVER be nervous again | Simon Sinek. From: https://www.youtube.com/watch?v=dqrZ3GDVf9s (2019-01-14).

Zvonimir Petricusic (2016) Harvey Specter #SUITS Best quotes. From: https://www.youtube.com/watch?v=WHW4sHMGohE (20190209)

Websites:

Dessin Animeforkids (2014) Pokemon S1 E1. From: https://www.youtube.com/watch?v=IB6ndZG8-YQ (2018-02-07)

English Oxford Dictionaries (w.y.) Act. From: https://en.oxforddictionaries.com/definition/action (2018-02-19)

English Oxford Dictionaries (w.y.) Behaviour. From: https://en.oxforddictionaries.com/definition/behaviour (2018-02-19)

English Oxford Dictionaries (w.y.) Butterfly effect. From: https://en.oxforddictionaries.com/definition/butterfly_effect (2019-02-08)

English Oxford Dictionaries (w.y) Cautious. From: https://en.oxforddictionaries.com/definition/cautious (2019-02-07)

English Oxford Dictionaries (w.y) Egotism. From: https://en.oxforddictionaries.com/definition/egotism (2019-02-07)

English Oxford living dictionaries (w.y) Enhusiasm. From: https://en.oxforddictionaries.com/definition/enthusiasm (2019-02-07)

English Oxford Dictionaries (w.y) Footprint. From: https://en.oxforddictionaries.com/definition/footprint (2019-02-09)

English Oxford living dictionaries (w.y) Identity crisis. From: https://en.oxforddictionaries.com/definition/identity_crisis (2019-02-07)

English Oxford Dictionaries (w.y) Manana. From: https://en.oxforddictionaries.com/definition/manana (2019-02-07)

English Oxford Dictionaries (w.y) Narcissism. From: https://en.oxforddictionaries.com/definition/narcissism (2019-02-07)

English Oxford living dictionaries (w.y) Passion. From: https://en.oxforddictionaries.com/definition/passion (2019-02-07)

English Oxford living dictionaries (w.y) Persistence. From: https://en.oxforddictionaries.com/definition/persistence (2019-02-07)

English Oxford living dictionaries (w.y) Success. From: https://en.oxforddictionaries.com/definition/success (2019-02-19)

English Oxford Dictionaries (w.y) Tabula rasa. From: https://en.oxforddictionaries.com/definition/tabula_rasa (2019-02-07)

Fandom (w.y) Family guy wiki. https://familyguy.fandom.com/wiki/Meg_Griffin (2019-02-07)

IMDb (w.y) How to get away with murder. From: https://www.imdb.com/title/tt3205802/ (2019-02-08)

IMDb (w.y) Latter days. From: https://www.imdb.com/title/tt0345551/?ref_=nv_sr_1 (2019-02-19) IMDb (w.y) Titanic. From: https://www.imdb.com/title/tt0120338/?ref_=ttmc_mc_tt (2019-02-09)

PCL open minds. (2016). Women More Than Twice as Likely to be Cautious about Risk than Men. From: http://www.psychological-consultancy.com/blog/women-twice-likely-cautious-risk-men/ (2019-01-14).

Pettit, H (2018). MailOnline: Tesla Roadster that Elon Musk sent into space could contaminate Mars with bacteria from Earth. From: https://www.dailymail.co.uk/sciencetech/article-5445857/Elon-Musks-Tesla-Roadster-contaminate-Mars.html (2019-01-14).

Rozental, A. (2014). Prokrastinering, stress och självmedkänsla. From: *http://www.psykologifabriken.se/prokrastinering-stress-och-sjalvmedkansla/* (2019-01-13).

Umiya Career Development Council (w.y) IQ EQ PQ AQ SQ CQ. From: http://jobs.ucdc.co.in/getpagedata.php?pageid=NDM%3D (2019-02-11).